Memphis

Juke Joints, Civil Rights, and Soulful Nights

Adam David

AMERICA
—
THROUGH
—
TIME

For my mom, who has always given me a home.

America Through Time
Fonthill Media LLC
www.through-time.com

First published 2025

ISBN 978-1-62545-160-6

Typeset in 9pt on 13pt Gotham
Printed and bound in England

All images were taken by the author unless otherwise noted.

Contents

About the Author   4

Introduction   5

1   The Best Thing About Beale Street? You Hear It Before You See It.   9

2   Around Town   33

3   Civil Rights   52

4   Clarksdale   62

5   Tom Lee Park   79

Epilogue   95

About the Author

Adam David moved to Memphis because he was fascinated with the city's culture, history, and unique community. His photography seeks to connect with emotion, humor, and compassion. His work has extensively captured his native New York, Washington, D.C., Havana, and Istanbul. He continues to live in Memphis, enjoying BBQ and live music as often as possible.

Introduction
Making the Home of
the Blues My Home

When Fonthill Media asked if I'd be interested in representing Memphis in their esteemed *Photographer's America* series, my first thought was, "Why me?"

That wasn't just a question of humility. Memphis has an incredible community of photographers, and I'd only lived in the city for under three years.

I'm originally from New York. I've also lived in Edinburgh, Washington D.C., Baltimore, and Phoenix. I visited Memphis in 2016 and 2018. On the first visit, I spent the bulk of my time taking day trips visiting nearby Clarksdale, Mississippi, and pursuing The Blues Trail. On the second, I went to even more remote areas of Mississippi like Money, Greenwood, and Avalon. But on each visit, I spent the nights on Beale Street soaking up live music and enjoying the scene.

I never considered moving to Memphis until my third visit in September 2020. I was living in Phoenix and working remotely due to the COVID-19 pandemic. In June, I had a bad case of COVID-19. After recovering, I reassessed many things. The most important was that I didn't want to plan for "someday" anymore. If there was something I wanted to do or accomplish, it was finally time to do it.

It was a Saturday night. I was in front of Blues City Café on Beale Street. And just like that, I found myself thinking, "I think I want to move here."

Fast forward to December. I packed the truck, left Phoenix, and haven't looked back.

So, what made me fall in love with Memphis?

The music, both past and present: If there wasn't Memphis, there wouldn't be Elvis. And if there wasn't Elvis, rock 'n' roll would never have had the impact on popular culture the way it did. Likewise, Stax Recording Studios and Royal Recording Studios made invaluable contributions to soul music with the likes of Otis Redding, Al Green, and Rufus Thomas. The music scene in Memphis continues to play a pivotal role in contemporary music. Artists like Three 6

Mafia, the late Gangsta Boo, and Yo Gotti are some of the most vibrant artists in popular music today.

The Grit: For the genre of photography that I study—street photography—it's favorable to have an urban environment with people walking, playing, and interacting. Downtown Memphis supplies all of these in abundance. Memphis is a visual wonder, with everything from pedestrians to street musicians to trollies and horse-drawn carriages up and down Main Street. Memphians are tough as nails but sweet as sugar. There's a unique Southern openness mixed with a sense of humor that is only born from struggle and being the constant underdog. Memphians understand their city is struggling with high crime rates. But if you need directions or roadside assistance, they're all heart. Heck, even if you give a smile to a stranger, nine times out of ten, they'll smile back.

The Culture: Memphians take a special pride in the town. They'll laugh at themselves, but they won't be the butt of anyone else's joke. If there's better BBQ anywhere on earth, I've yet to taste it. You'll never find more rabid fans of their home team than Grizzlies fans. And everybody in this town has a creative side. Whether they're musicians, digital artists, or dancers, artistic expression flourishes here. It reminds me of Brooklyn or New York's Lower East Side when I was growing up: affordable enough for artists to live in with enough culture and clubs to give them sustenance. Memphis went from roadside Juke Joints playing blues to Jookin', an African American street dance.

Local and Nearby Historical Sites: Seminal blues figures such as Muddy Waters, John Lee Hooker, and Pinetop Perkins hail from the region surrounding Clarksdale, MS, a mere 75 miles away. Clarksdale is also the home of the Legend of the Crossroads—where the musician Robert Johnson supposedly sold his eternal soul to the Devil for fame and fortune—and the annual Juke Joint Festival, where every April music fans and musicians from all over the world descend on the town to celebrate the music they love.

Likewise, many other historical markers are nearby: Berclair (birthplace of B. B. King), Vicksburg (the site of one of the Civil War's most consequential battles), and Money (where Emmett Till's tragic murder in 1955 launched the Civil Rights Movement) are all over the state border in Mississippi and a day trip away.

So, with all this amazing and diverse culture and talent, why pick someone so new to the town to represent it? I have a theory about that.

To be a photographer, you must be a part of a place. However, you also—importantly—must be *apart* from it. In other words, you need to know the place like the back of your hand, but you must simultaneously be arm's length from it. Knowing the place is the only way to dig below the surface, but you also need to be not so familiar with it that you overlook the magic. I go out most nights to photograph things. Somehow, I constantly stumble on something new—even when I've walked that same ground and stood at that location dozens of times.

And maybe that's the difference: I am a New Yorker experiencing Memphis as both an insider and an outsider.

Many Memphians never take advantage of the incredible opportunities they have at their fingertips. The same happened for me and New York. I reached a point where I took the city for granted. I didn't feel the need to go to Central Park on any given day, visit the Twin Towers, or go to St. Mark's Place. You think those things have always been there, so they always will be. Or will they? Central Park is different than it used to be. The Twin Towers were lost, though the Freedom Tower and the Oculus are gorgeous. And St. Mark's is no longer the home of punk music and downtown dive bars but upscale restaurants and pricey nightclubs.

One big difference between New York and Memphis is the amount of foot traffic. In New York, there are always people everywhere you go. That's not the case in Memphis. For street photography, that can sometimes be frustrating. Some days, there aren't many subjects out and about to shoot. That comparative scarcity also means that, as a photographer, it's harder to get lost in the crowd. If a subject sees you aim your camera in their direction without permission, it might not be appreciated.

But, as my high school science teacher would say, sometimes the problem is the solution. Interacting with and asking a subject for permission to take the picture results in a kind of photography much more difficult to achieve in New York.

I told a close friend about this book. She said it best: "Thinking about Memphis street photography vs New York. I am not sure what your selections will be, but what I like best about your photography in Memphis is the openness of some of your subjects, looking straight into the camera, enjoying your company, and being photographed doing whatever it is they are doing. I'm used to street photography aiming to capture the oblivious, so I appreciate that your subjects seem joyous and engaged, and that's Memphis."

I couldn't have said it better.

Memphis is constantly evolving. And, as Steve Earle (who recorded his seminal album Copperhead Road at Memphis's own Ardent Studios) once sang: "One thing change will bring is something new." This collection of photographs captures where Memphis is today, with a sense of where it's going. The optimism and hope of the people—despite significant odds—make me confident that better days are ahead, with the commitment to retain the unique soul, gritty resilience, and incredible spirit of the Home of the Blues.

The founder of Sun Studios, Sam Philips, said these words about Howlin' Wolf, but they equally apply to Memphis: "This is where the soul of man never dies."

I'm honored Fonthill Media has provided this opportunity to showcase my Memphis. I hope you enjoy it.

1

The Best Thing About Beale Street? You Hear It Before You See It.

You'll see pretty browns in beautiful gowns
You'll see tailor-mades and hand-me-downs
You'll meet honest men, and pick-pockets skilled
And business never ceases 'til somebody gets killed

W. C. Handy, "Beale Street Blues"

Memphis has many nicknames: "The 901," after the area code; "Grind City," for its beloved basketball team, the Grizzlies; and "Bluff City," because of its high bluffs above the flood levels of the Mississippi River.

But its most enduring and affectionate nickname is "The Home of the Blues." And for good reason. The sound of guitars, drums, and singing emanates across Beale Street's surrounding blocks. If you're a music fanatic, Beale Street is as close to heaven as it gets.

And that's just a prelude to arriving on the block and seeing it: the neon lights, the crowds of locals and visitors, and the gritty, sloping street. The names of the venues say it all: Blues City Café. B. B. King's Blues Club. Blues Hall. Rum Boogie Café. I come down to Beale Street at least three times a week. I always have the same excited feeling, but every time is a completely different, exhilarating experience.

Beale Street was established in 1841. In the wake of the Civil War's Battle of Memphis in 1862, thousands of enslaved African Americans escaped from Mid-South farms and plantations and came to Memphis and the area around it. As a result, Beale Street became a commercial and cultural hub for Memphis's African American community for decades.

Beale Street played a crucial role in America's Civil Rights struggle. In 1892, Ida B. Wells began publishing the anti-segregationist newspaper Free Speech from the historic First Baptist Church—an apt location since the church was built by a congregation of formerly enslaved people. In 2021, a statue was erected to honor her accomplishments.

Arguably, Beale Street's most vital cultural legacy is music. W. C. Handy, known as "The Father of the Blues," wrote "Beale Street Blues," celebrating the strange, unique alchemy of the street. Beale Street is Ground Zero for developing the style known as Memphis Blues. Local and national blues and jazz figures who helped shape and mold the style include Bukka White, B. B. King, Louis Armstrong, Muddy Waters, Albert King, Memphis Minnie, Rufus Thomas, Rosco Gordon, Furry Lewis, and others.

One white teenager from Tupelo, Mississippi, was greatly inspired by the music he heard on Beale. The influence of the music Elvis Presley heard and fell in love with while hanging around the clubs and parlors on Beale in the 1950s cannot be overestimated. It would directly tie to the cultural explosion of rock 'n' roll music.

In addition to blues, Memphis is also home to Stax Records, where Otis Redding, Isaac Hayes, and Booker T. & the MG's revolutionized soul music. Royal Studios is where Al Green and Willie Mitchell created a different, competing form of soul music. And, of course, it's impossible to overlook the importance of Sun Studios, where Sam Phillips recorded Howlin' Wolf, The Prisonaires, Jerry Lee Lewis, Johnny Cash, Carl Perkins, Rosco Gordon, and—of course—the King himself, Elvis Presley. For all, Beale Street played a major role in their musical inspiration and influence.

In 1964, the Memphis Housing Authority (MHA) released an urban renewal plan to transform Beale Street from a local neighborhood to a tourist attraction. Hundreds of people, buildings, and businesses were displaced. But by 1973, MHA's funding had run out, and Beale deteriorated and was largely abandoned.

It wasn't until Elvis Presley's death that Memphis became a tourist attraction again. Fans from all over the world were coming to visit Graceland. The city recognized an opportunity to revitalize Beale Street to satiate the tourists' appetite for local culture and nightlife.

Today, Beale Street thrives with an array of clubs and restaurants. Locals and visitors love the world-class music pumping from the bars. Restaurants like Blues City Café, which proudly proclaims, "Put Some South in Yo' Mouth!" serve local favorites like BBQ, fried catfish, and gumbo. On weeknights in the warmer months, the street hosts "Hot Rods on Beale," "Antique Car Night," "Bike Night," and more. And there isn't a better place to be when locals leave the nearby FedExForum after a Grizzlies win and flood Beale to celebrate.

The last of the blues legends still play regularly—Blind Mississippi Morris, Earl "The Pearl" Banks—and an array of younger musicians with newer styles are also making their mark. With all that said, can pictures do Beale Street justice? The cliché goes that a picture says a thousand words—but can a photo capture the music and nightlife up and down Beale, where every night is Saturday night?

Only one way to find out! Put on your most rock 'n' roll outfit, make sure you have your credit card handy, and get ready to have one of the greatest nights of your life: we're heading for The Home of the Blues!

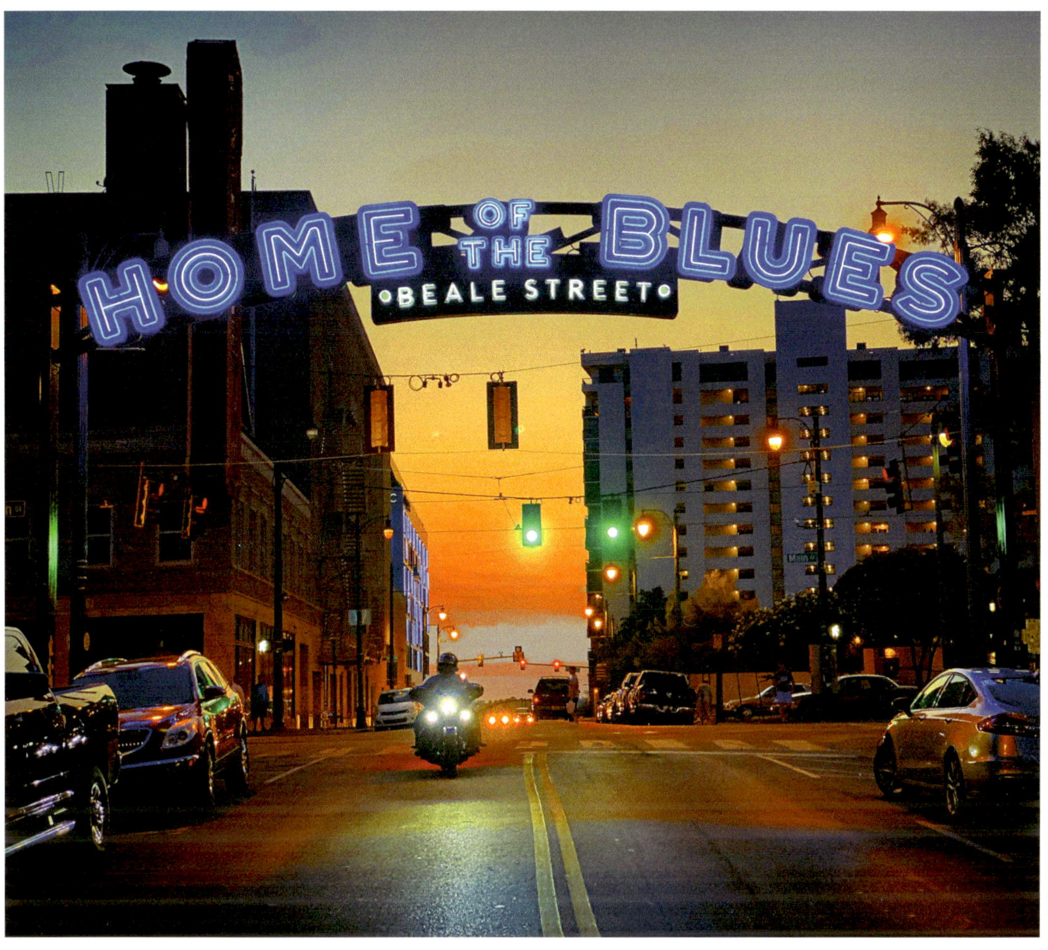

The sight of that sign and sunset never gets old.

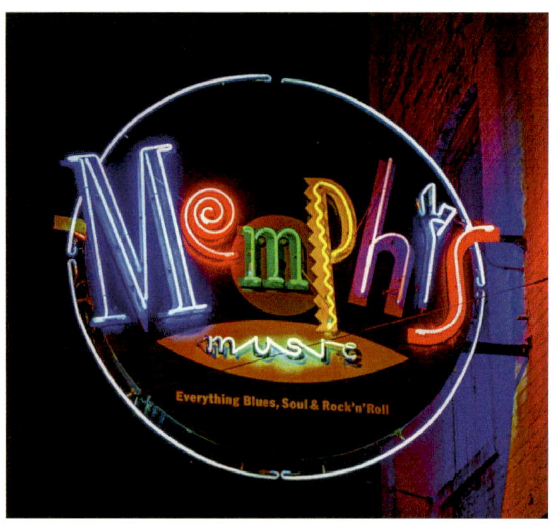

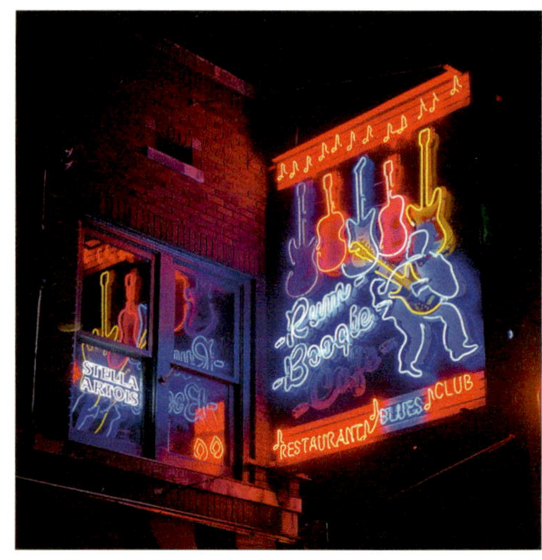

Beale Street's neon signs are like a homecoming for music lovers.

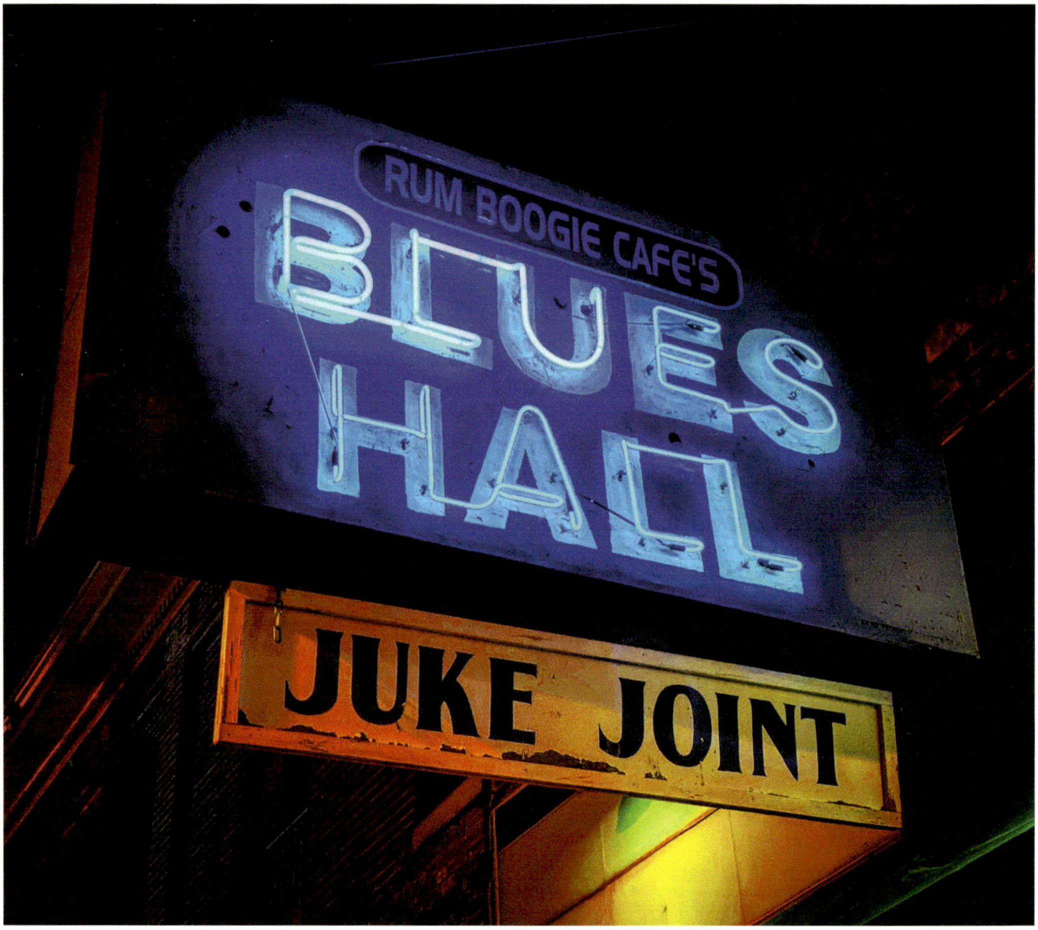

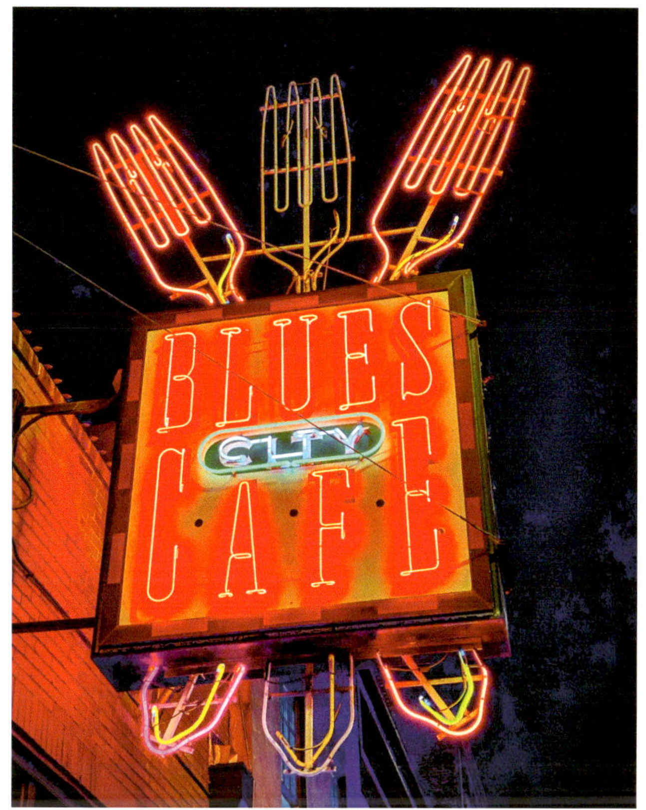
BLUES
CITY
CAFE

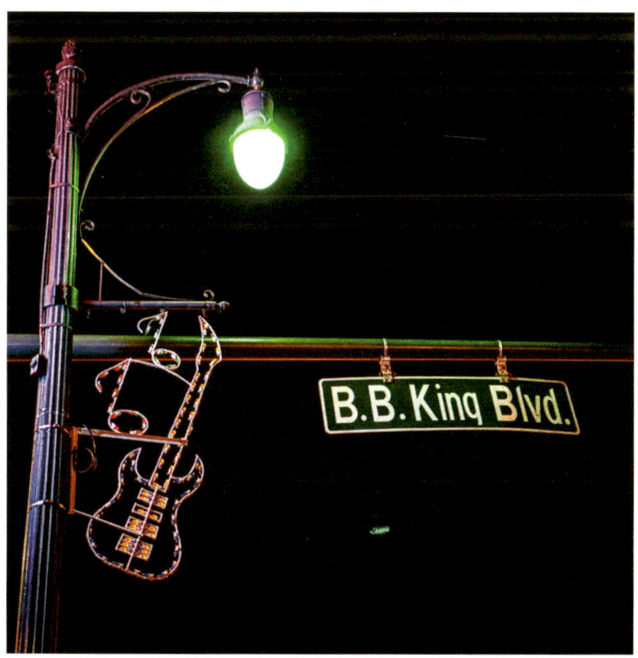
B.B. King Blvd.

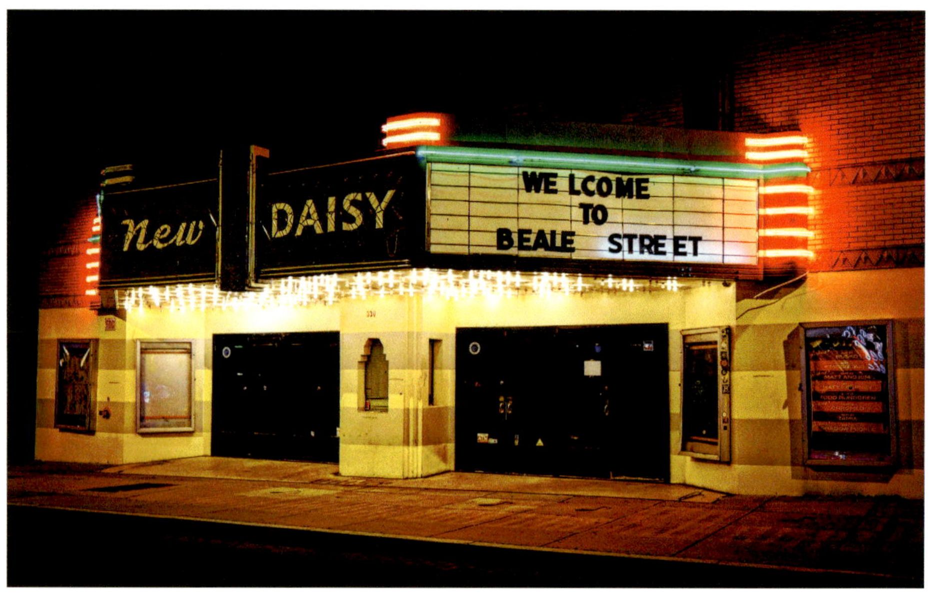
New DAISY
WELCOME
TO
BEALE STREET

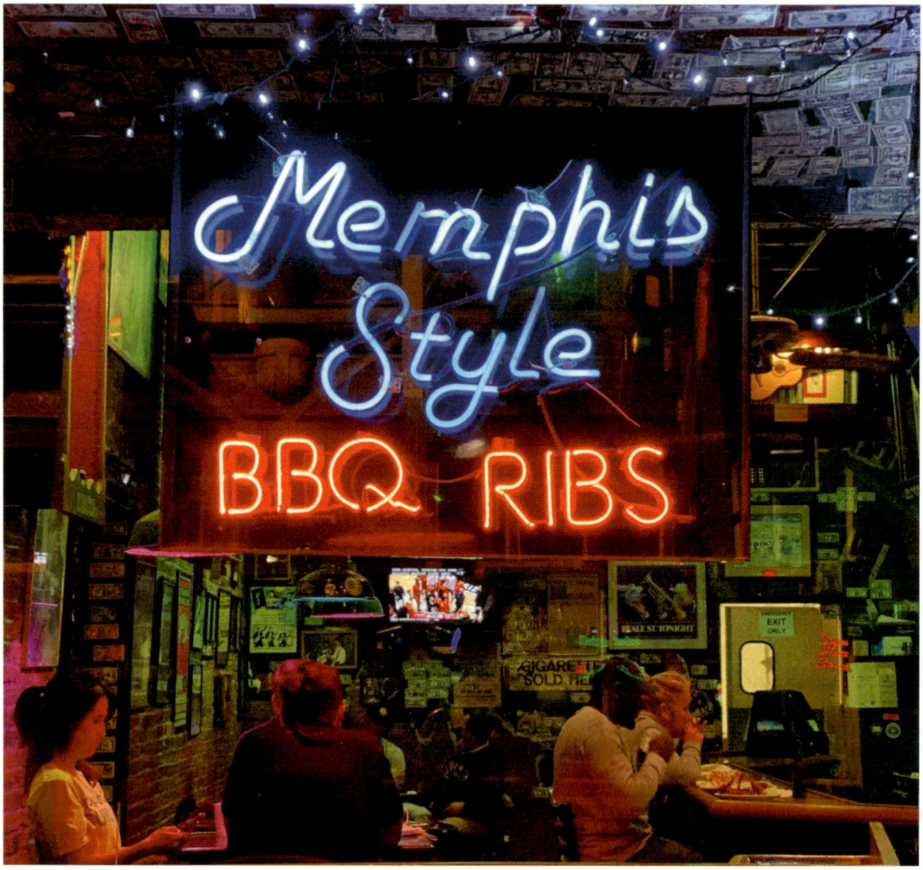

Memphis
Style
BBQ RIBS

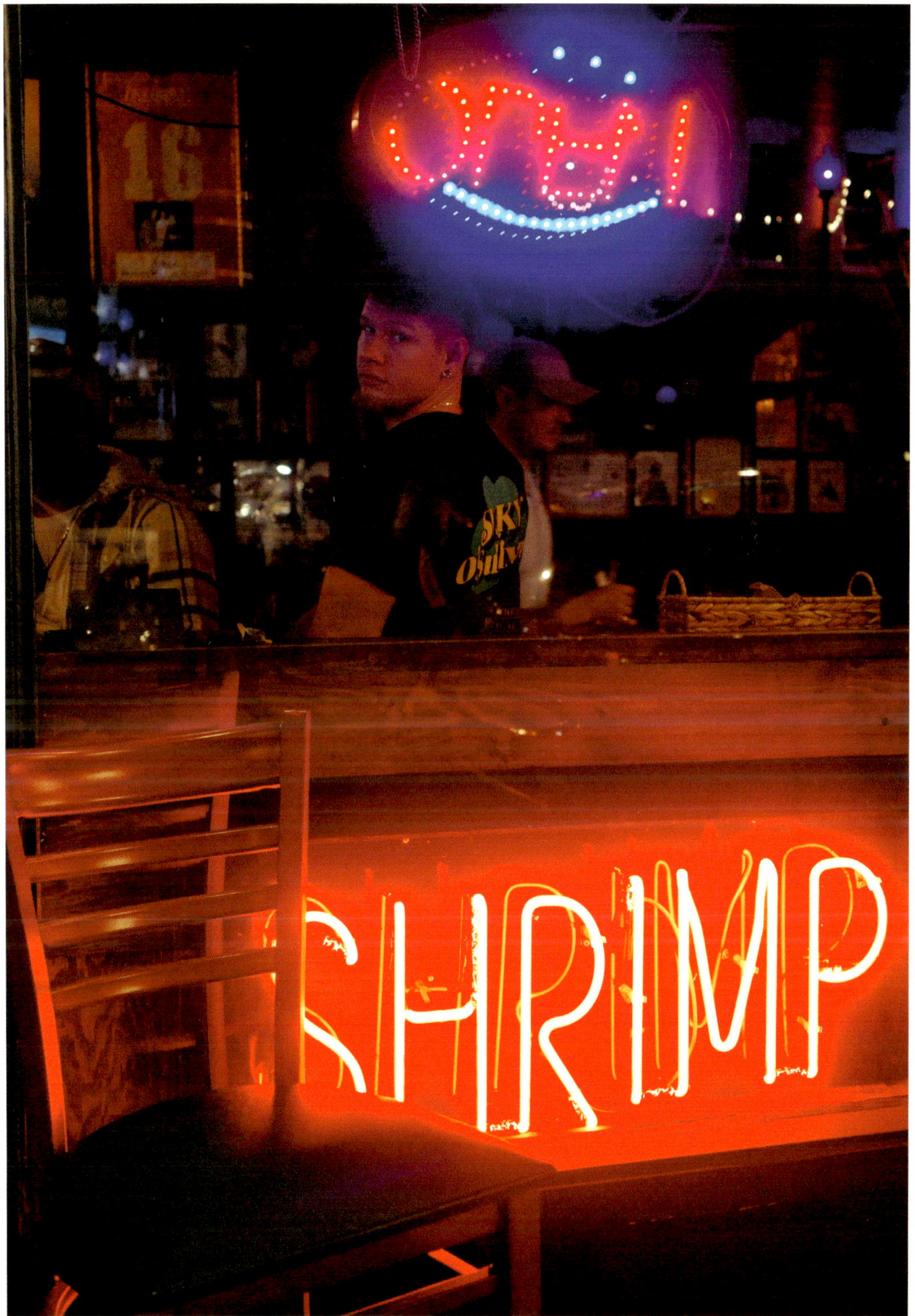
SHRIMP

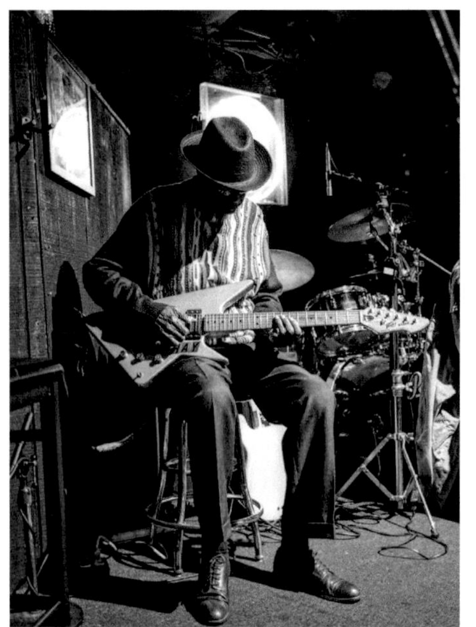

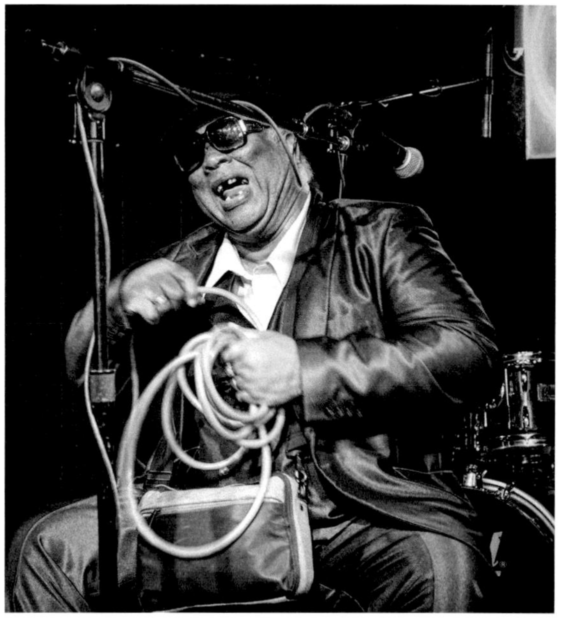

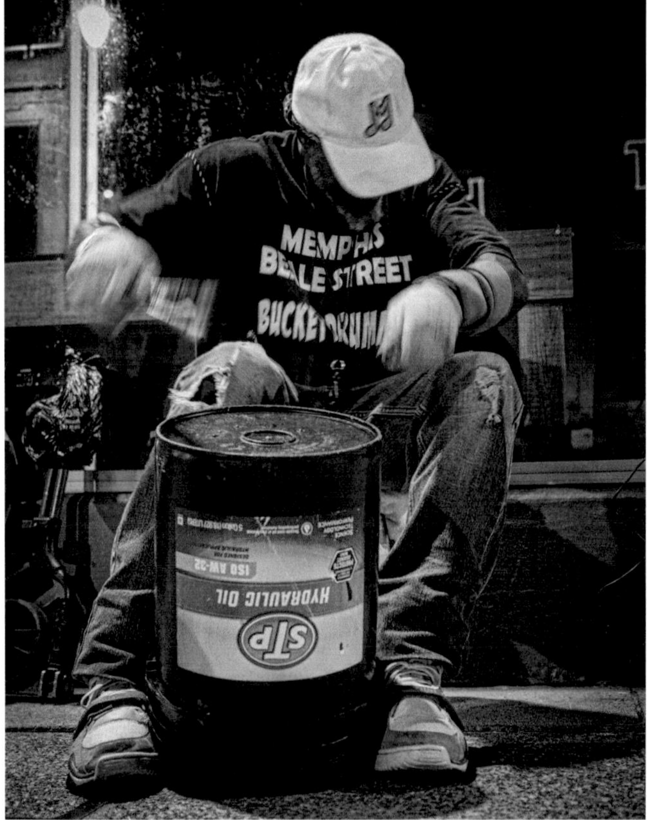

Above left: Blues legend, Earl "The Pearl" Banks.

Above right: Blues legend, Blind Mississippi Morris.

Left: Lomax, Beale Street bucket drummer extraordinaire.

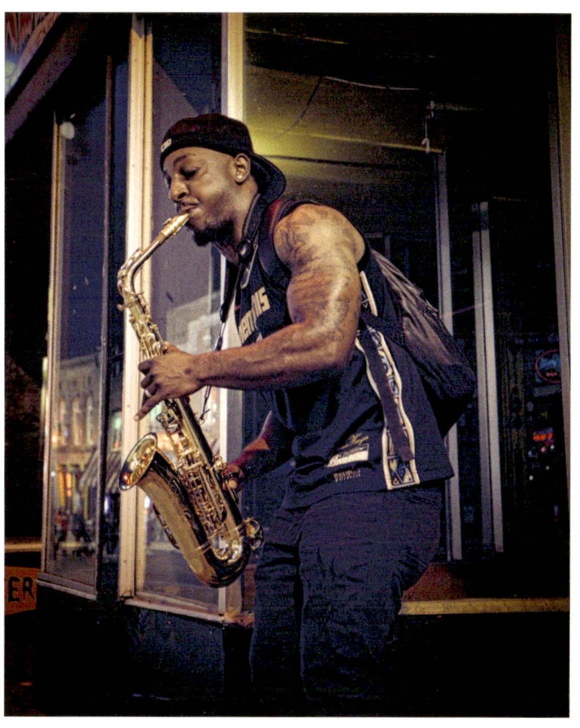

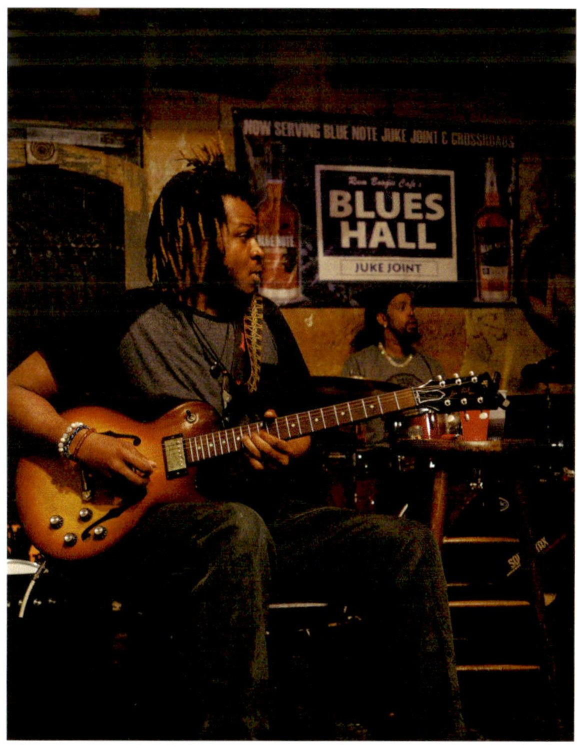

Music emanates from
the streets and bars.

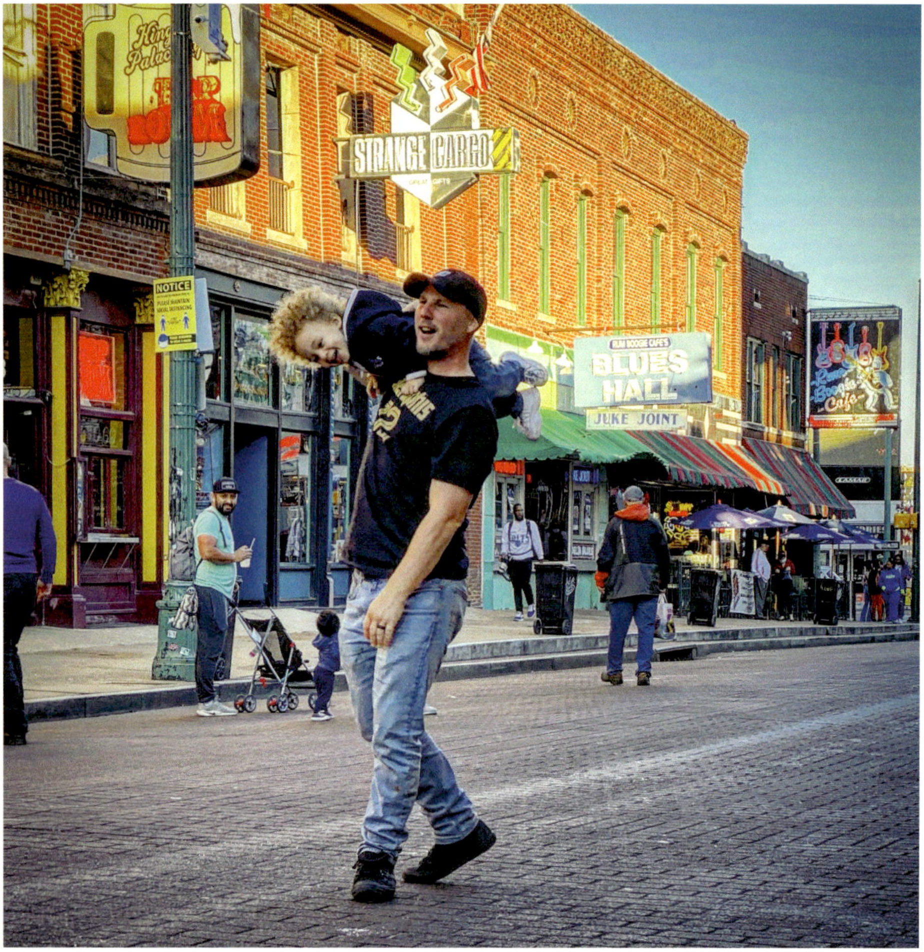

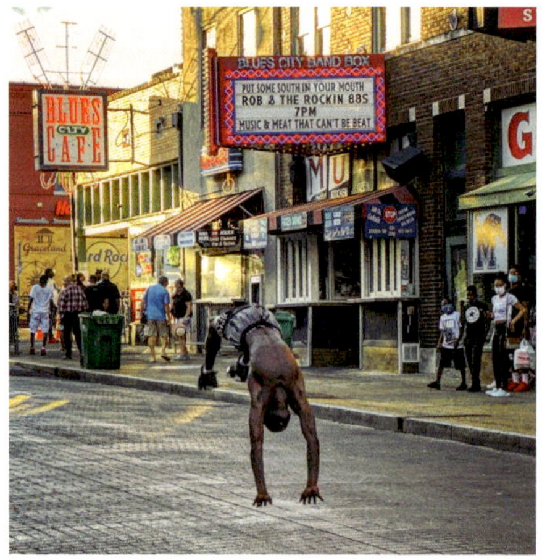

Above and below: Whether you're flipping your kid or being entertained by the Beale Street Flippers, during the day Beale Street is filled with family fun.

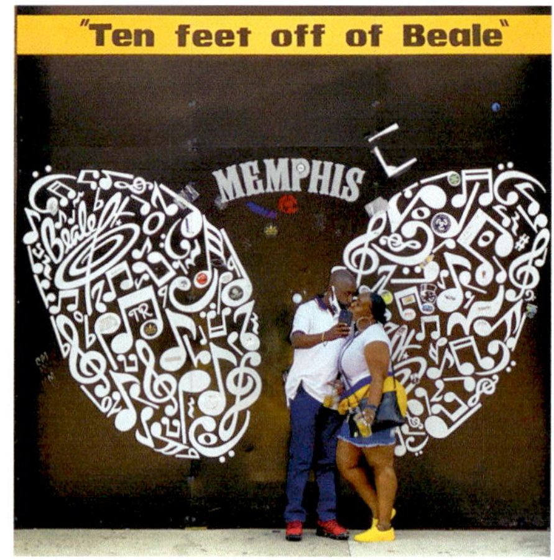

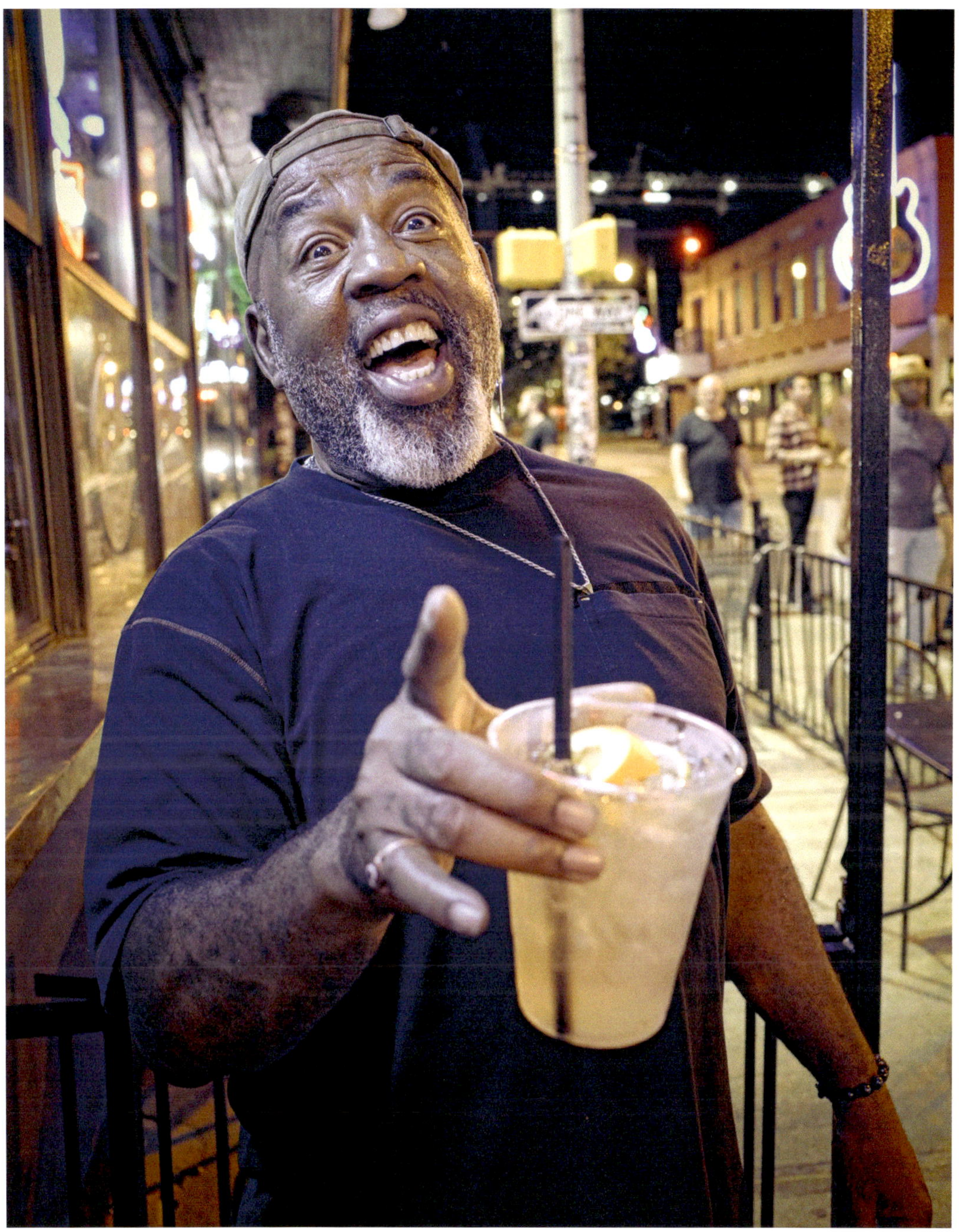

But the nightlife is what Beale Street is all about.

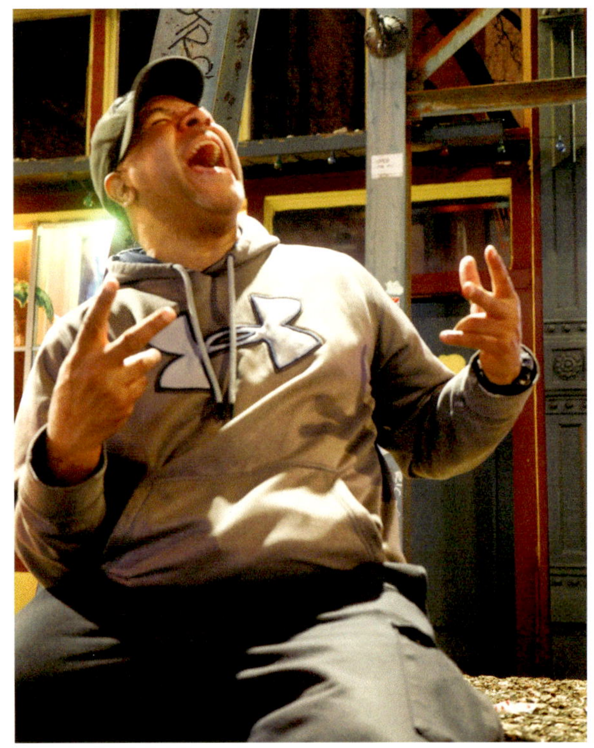

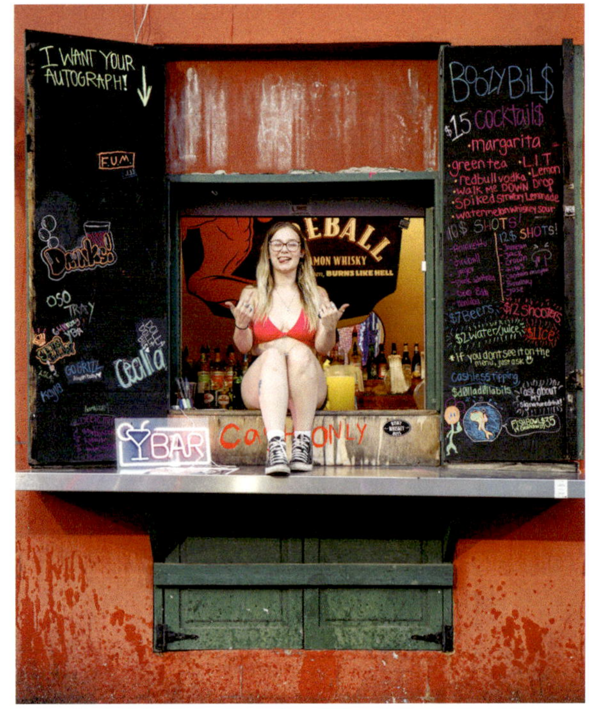

I WANT YOUR AUTOGRAPH!
BOOZY BIL$
$15 COCKTAIL$
margarita
green tea
redbull vodka
walk me DOWN
Spiked Lemonade
watermelon whiskey sour
L.I.T
Lemon Drop
10$ SHOTS!
12$ SHOTS!
$7 BEERS
$12 Shooters
$2 water/juice
CASH ONLY
YBAR

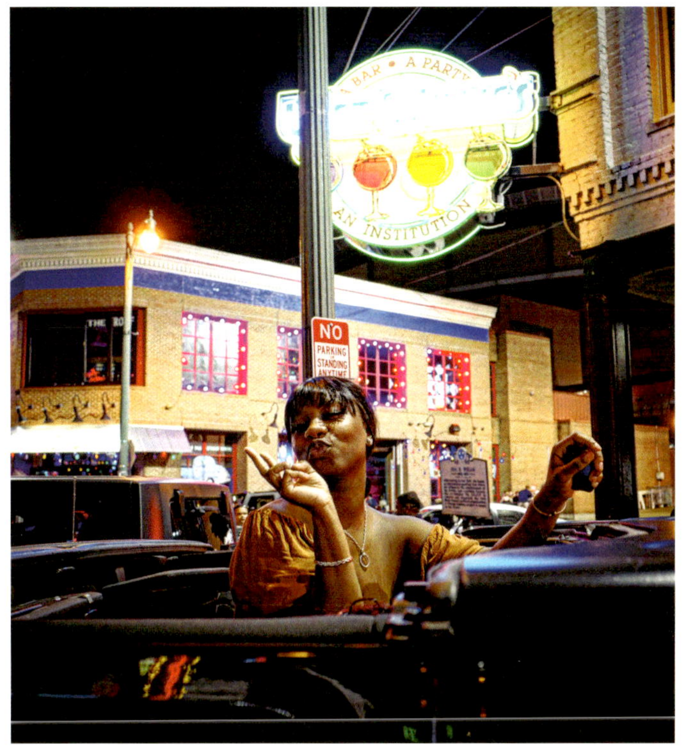

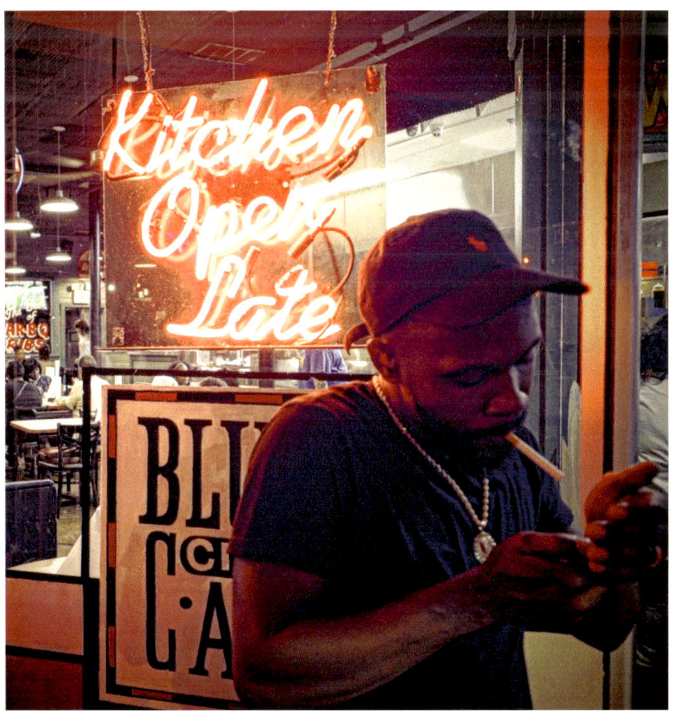

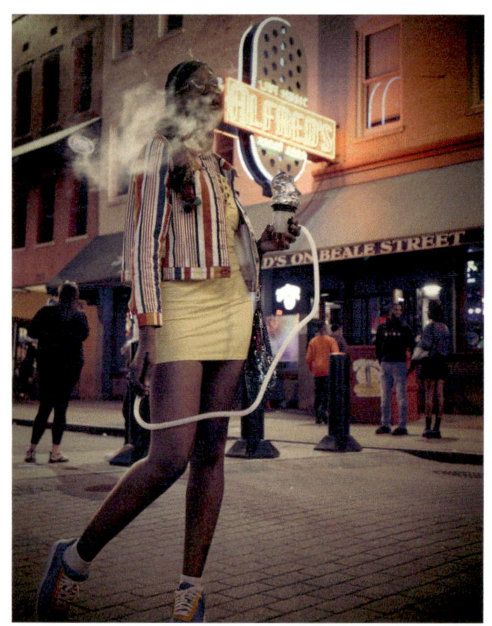

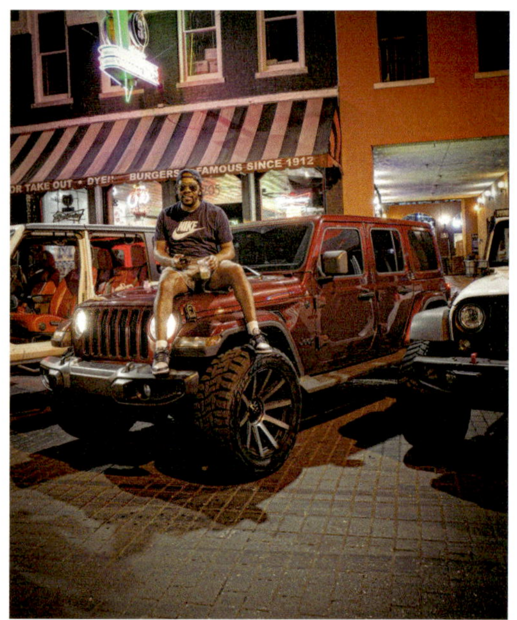

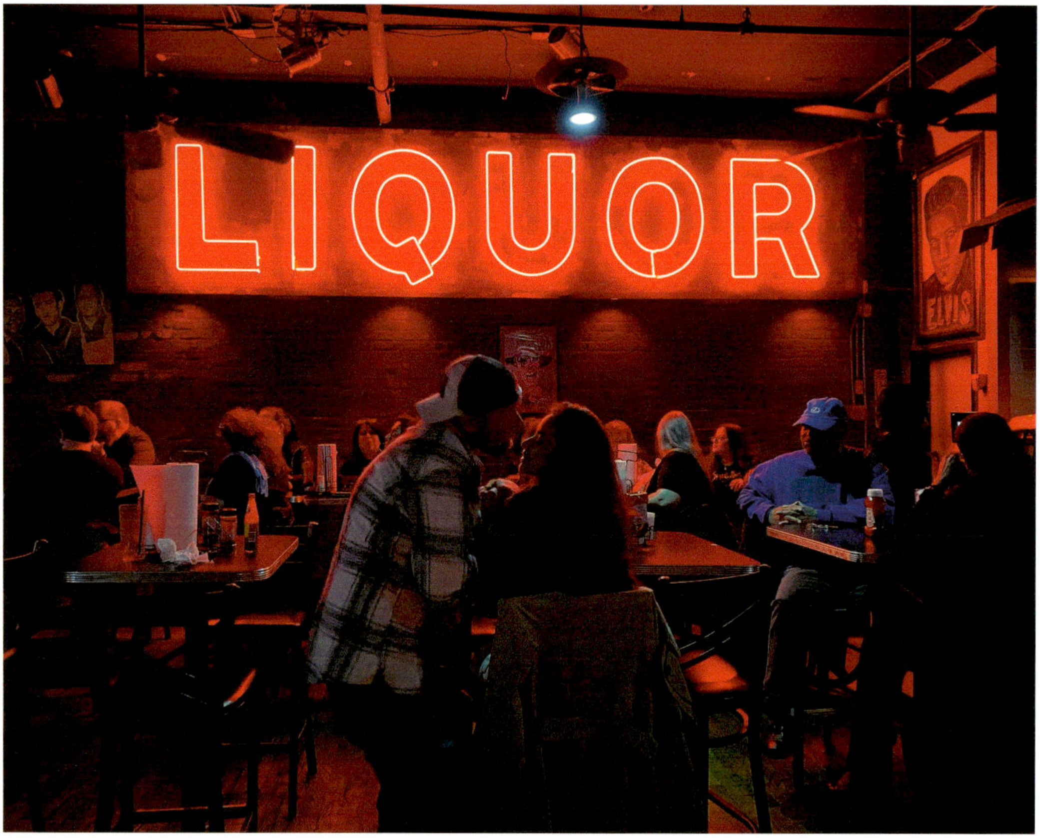

LIQUOR
ELVIS

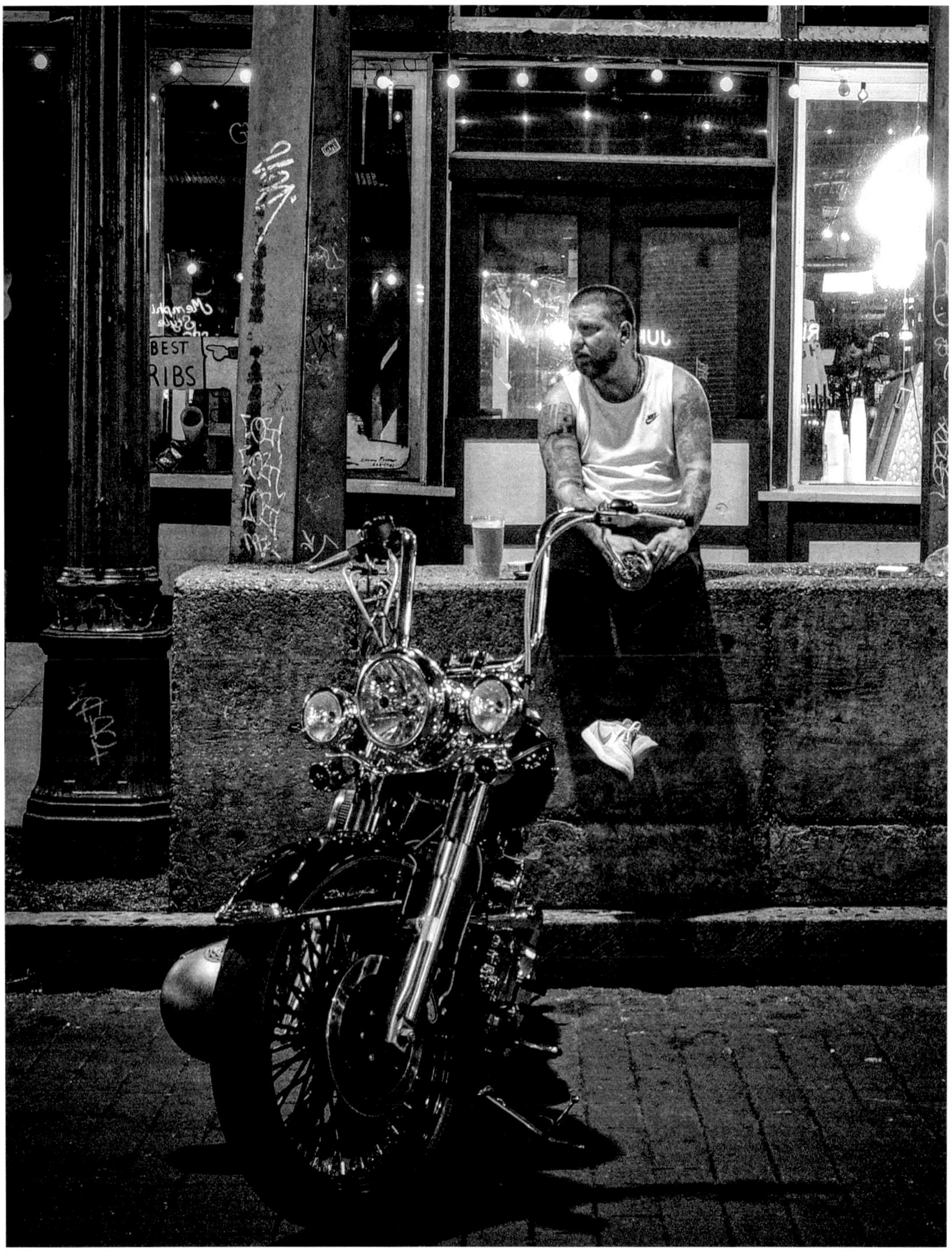

During the warmer months, Wednesday Night is Bike Night on Beale. The street fills with local and visiting bikers. It's always a great time.

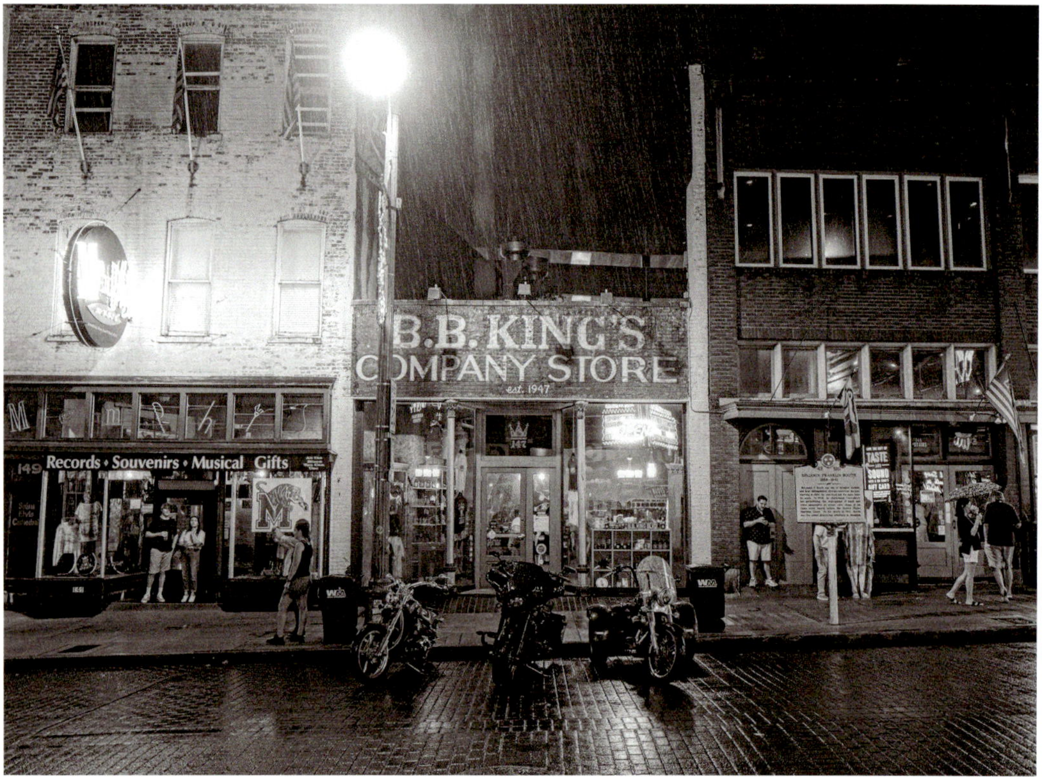

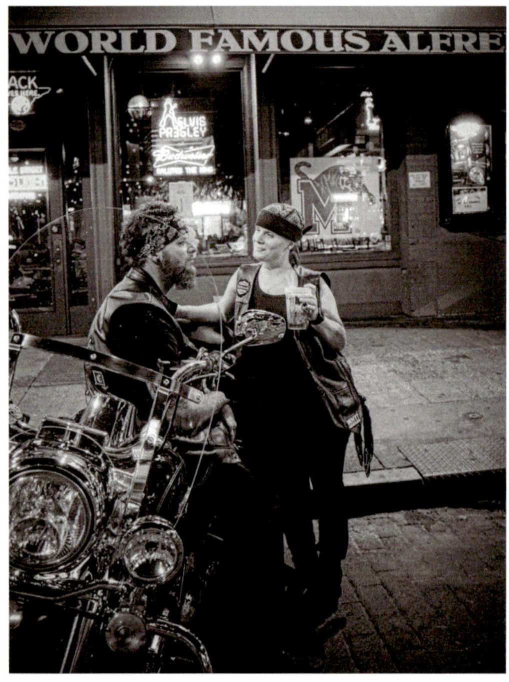

WORLD FAMOUS ALFRE

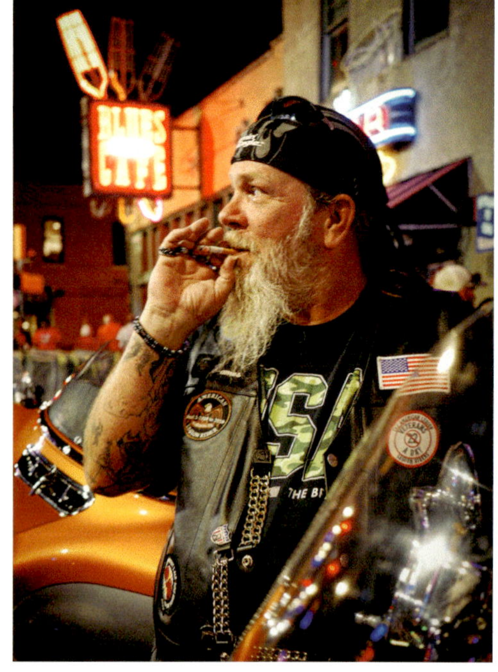

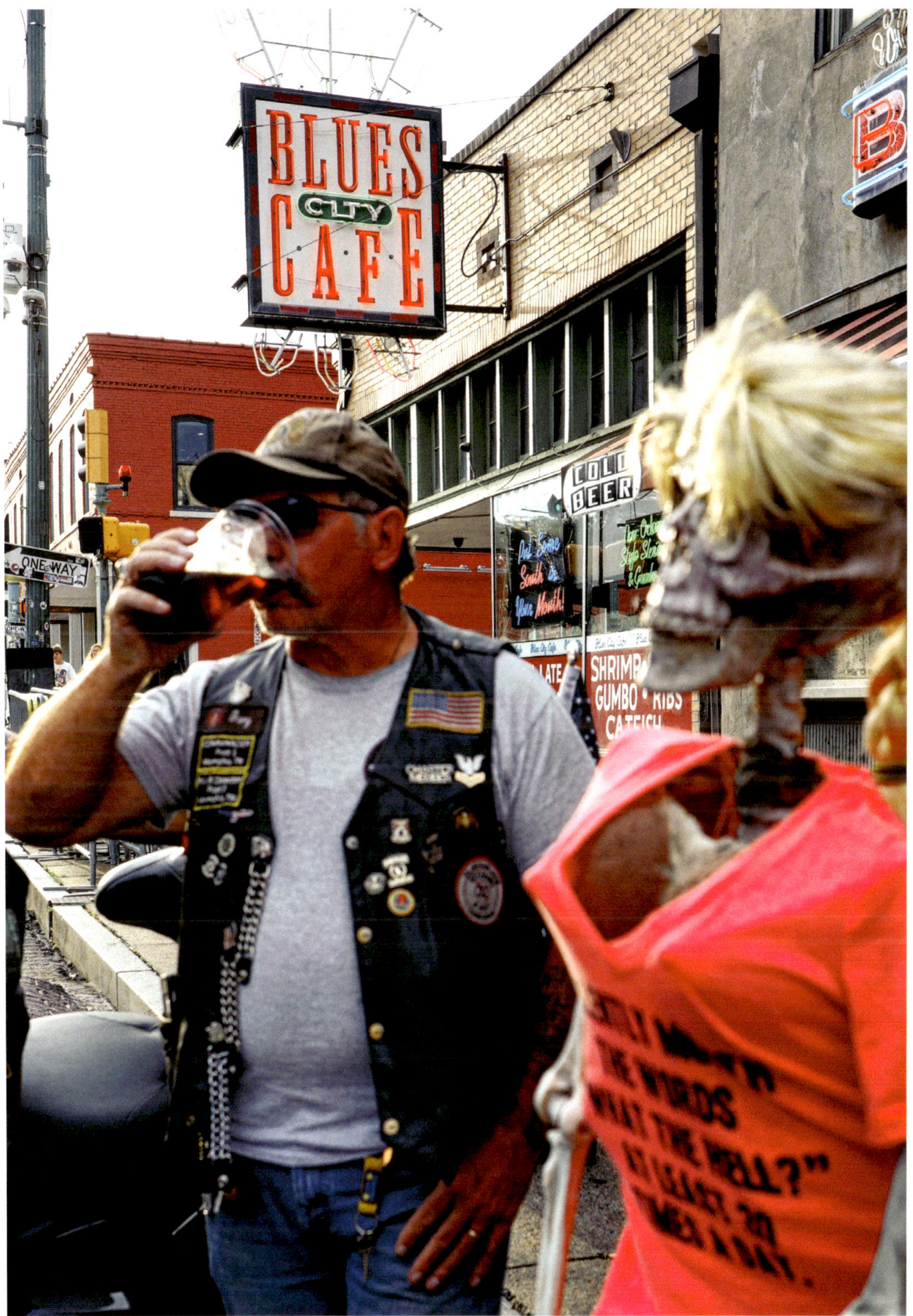
BLUES
CITY
CAFE
COLD
BEER
SHRIMP
GUMBO • RIBS
CATFISH
ONE WAY
THE WORDS
WHAT THE HELL?"

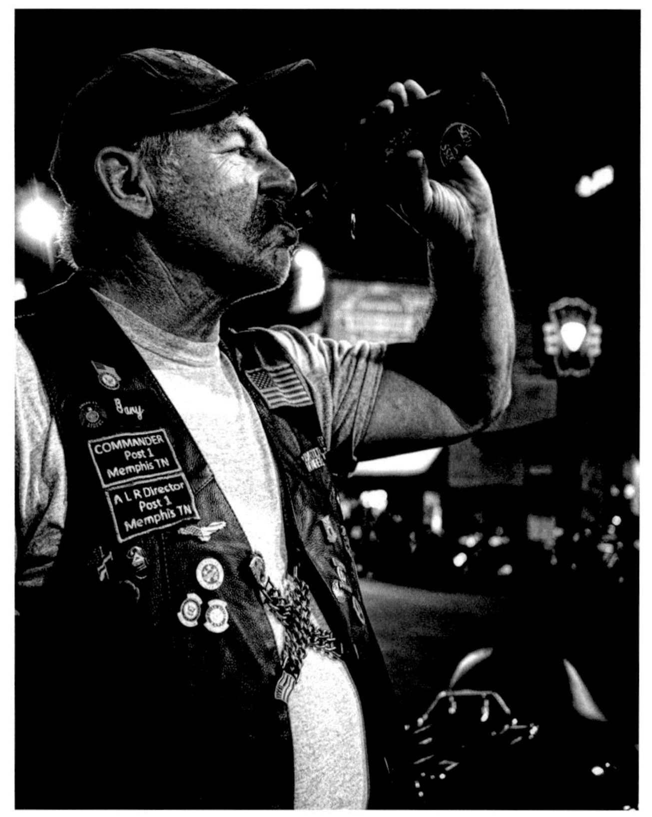

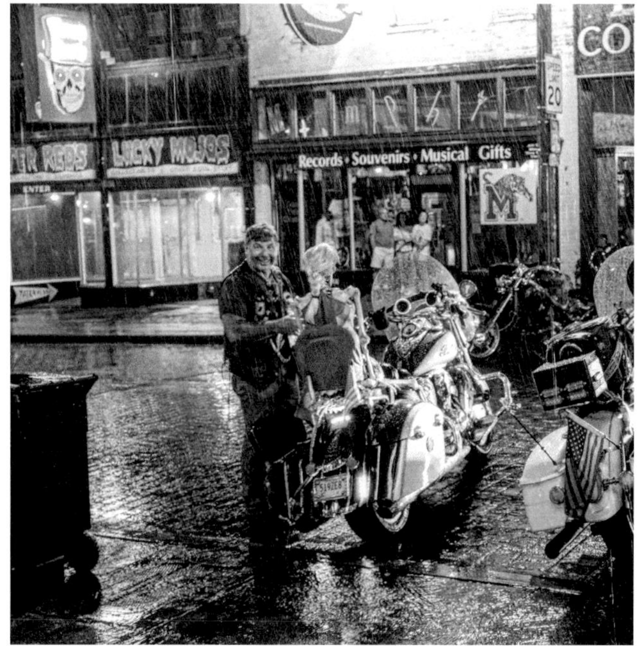

LUCKY MOJOS
Records • Souvenirs • Musical • Gifts
CO
SPEED LIMIT 20
M

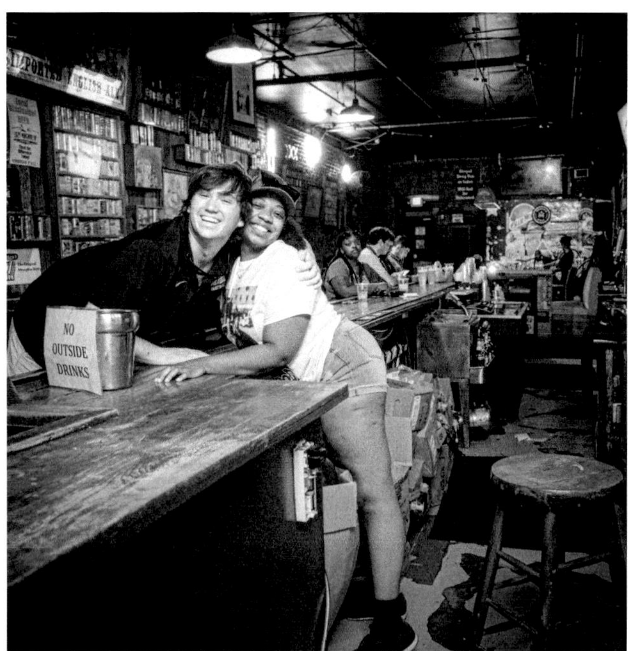

Beale Street sells smiles.

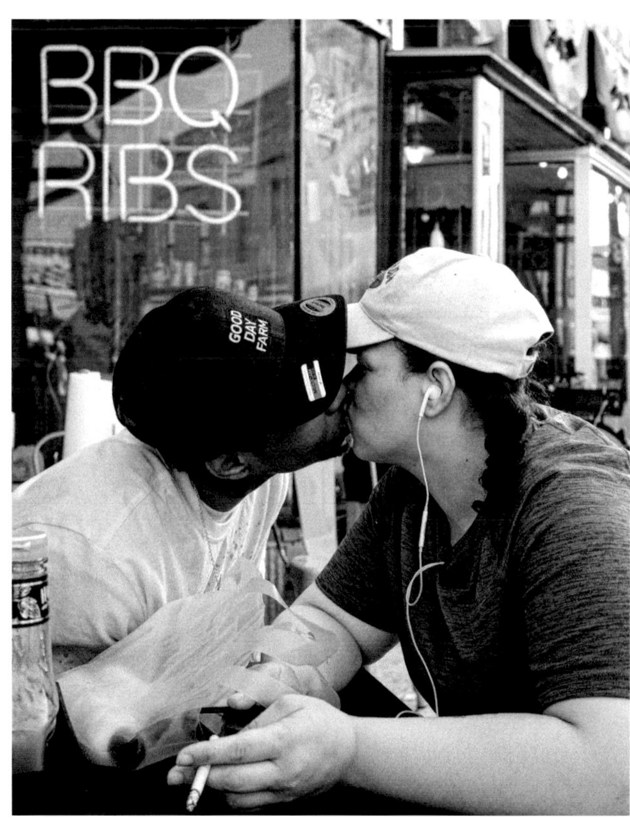

The only thing better than BBQ and a cigarette is a post-BBQ kiss while having a smoke.

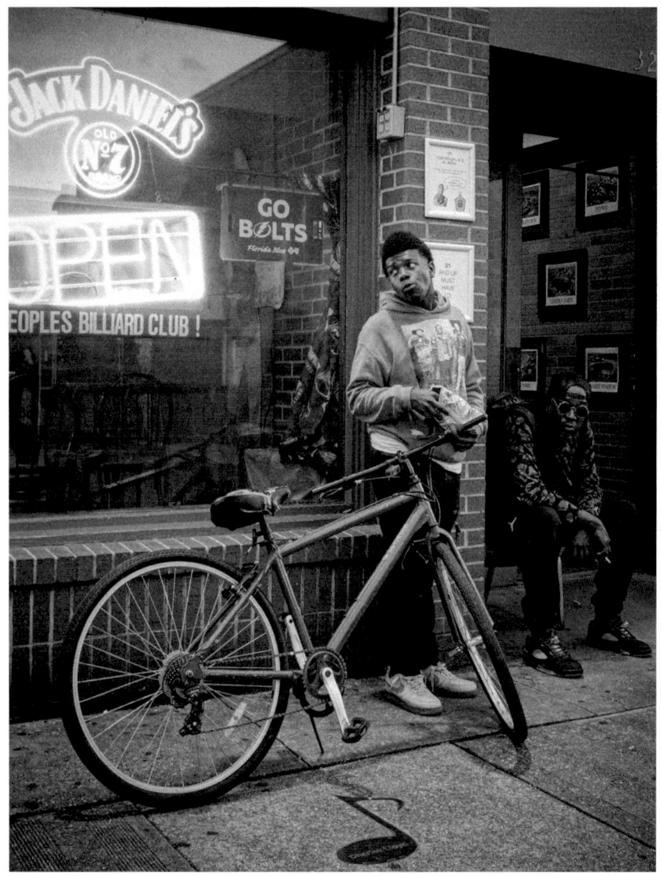

Left: People's Pool Hall.

Below: If you stay out late enough, Beale gets its freak on.

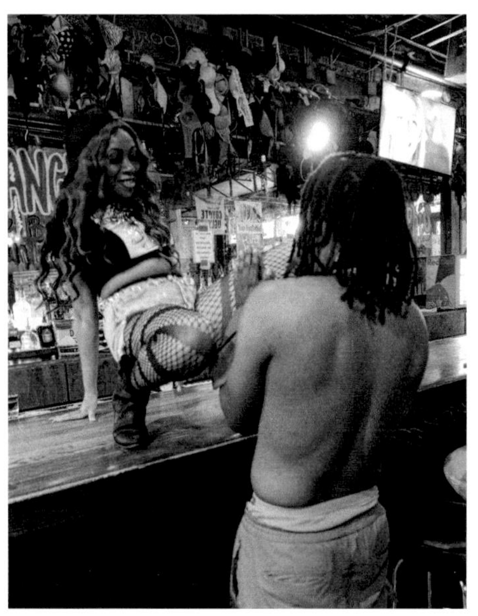

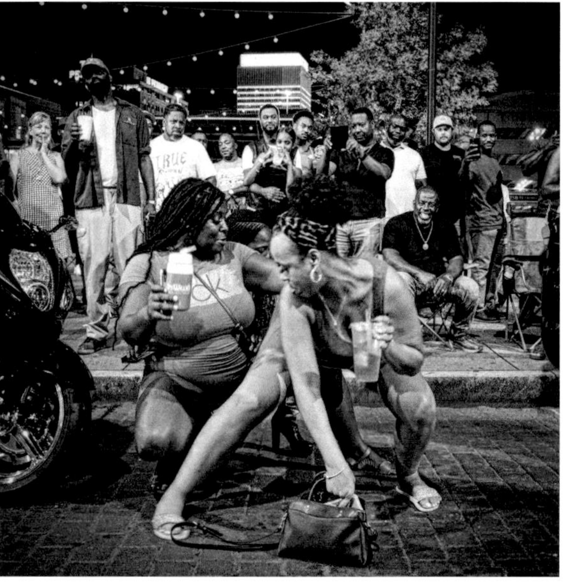

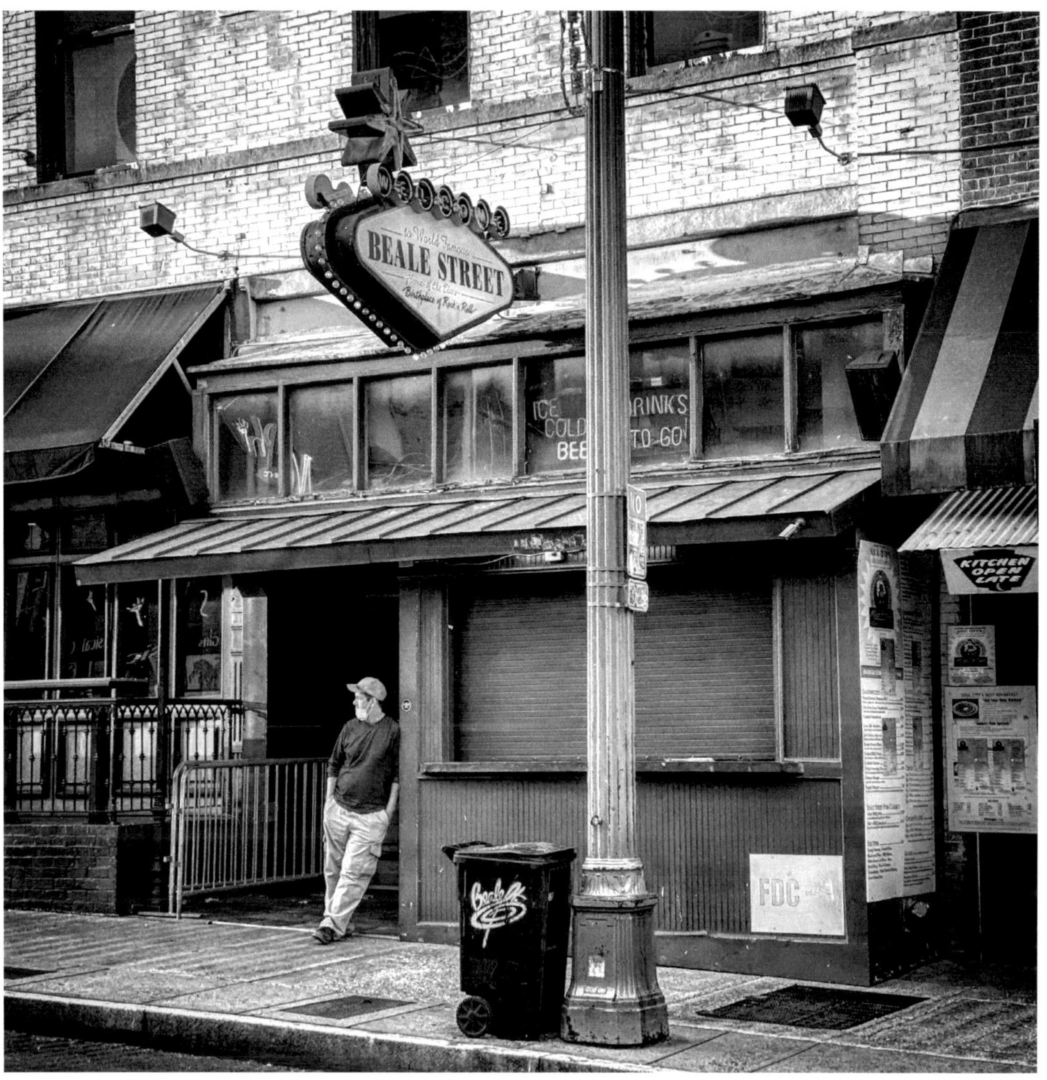

Blue & Lonesome.

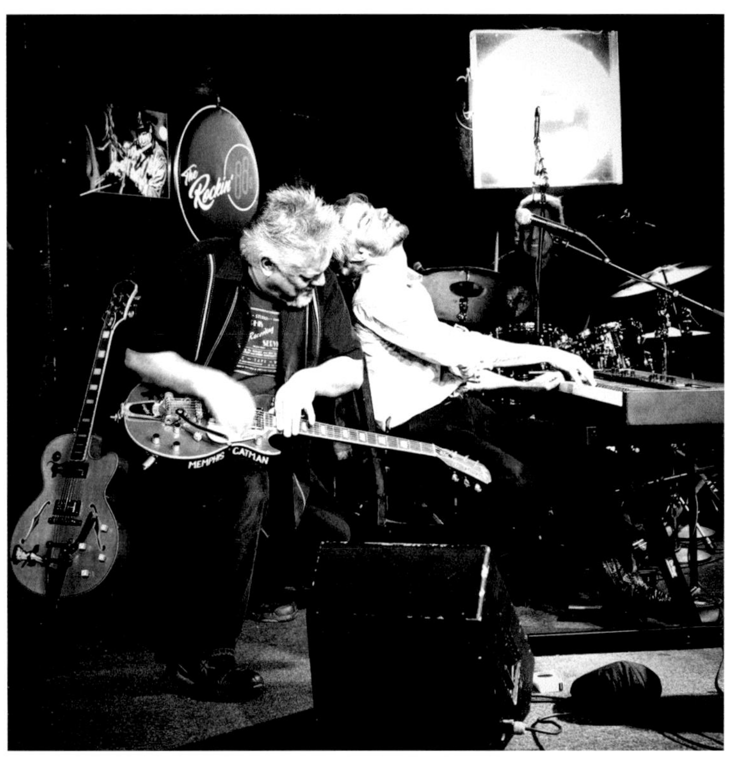

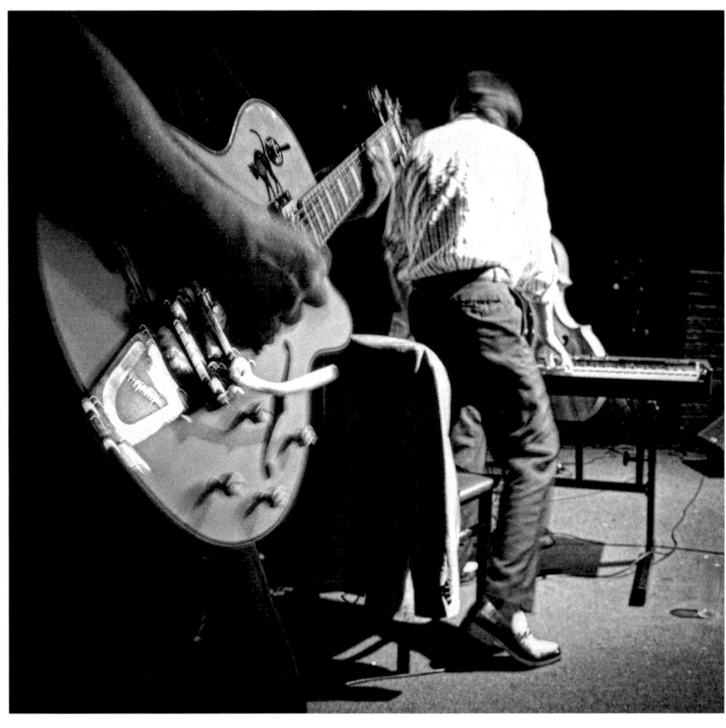

The Rockin' 88s.

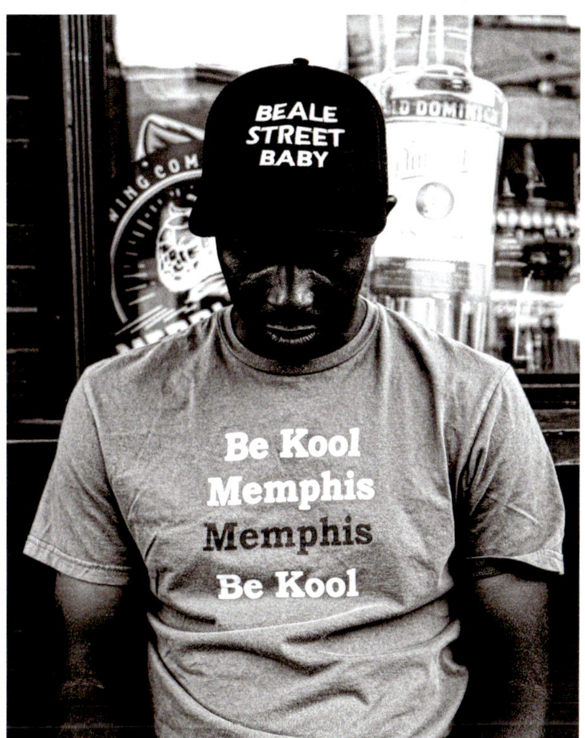

Right: Nat Hewlett, the Godfather of Beale.

Below: Elvis's statue in the blizzard of 2021.

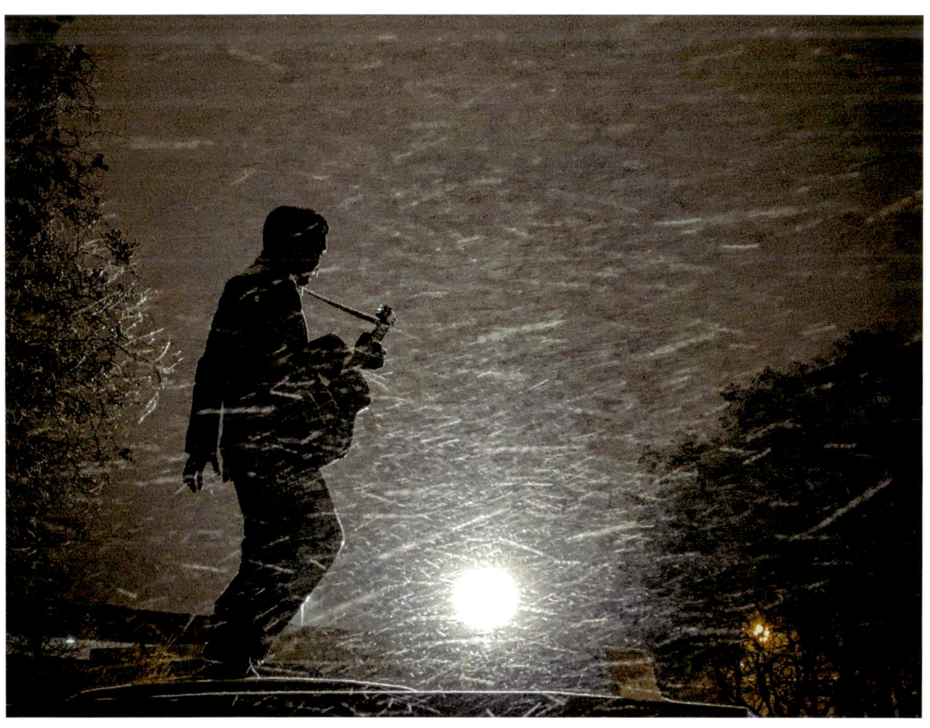

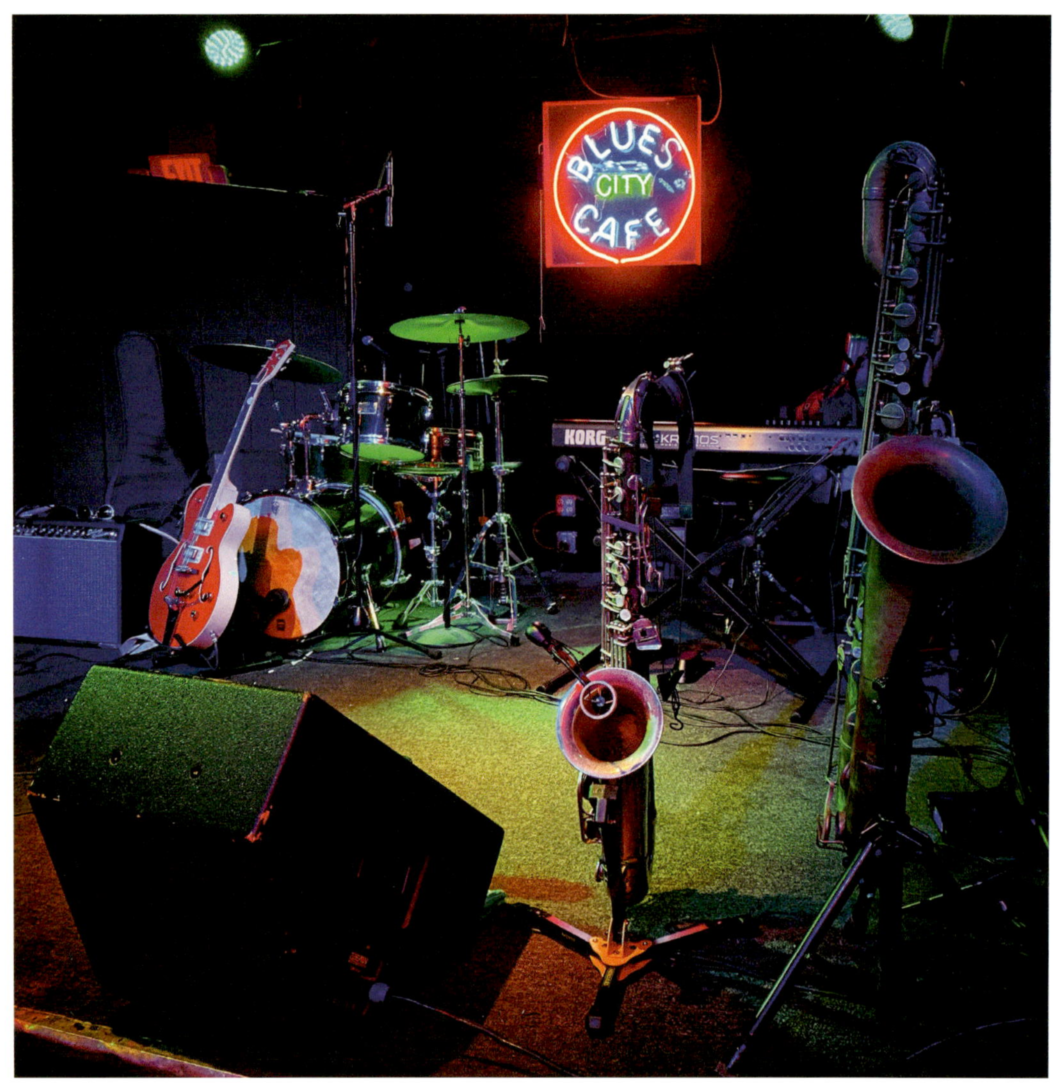

On Beale, the music stops but never ends.

2

Around Town

The same week I moved to Memphis in December 2020, the news reported that a man playing saxophone had been arrested in Overton Park for the charge of indecent exposure. The comments immediately flooded in: "It's Memphis. Of course there's a naked man in the park playing sax!" I immediately knew I had made the right choice moving here and would fit right in.

Memphians have one of the oddest senses of humor I've ever encountered. It's different than New York's cynicism, sharper than Baltimore's world-weariness, and much more celebratory of the city's eccentricities than D.C. or Phoenix.

From signs around town to public displays of art to transforming a brothel into a haunted dive bar serving the best burgers you've ever had, Memphis is weird, wild, and wonderful.

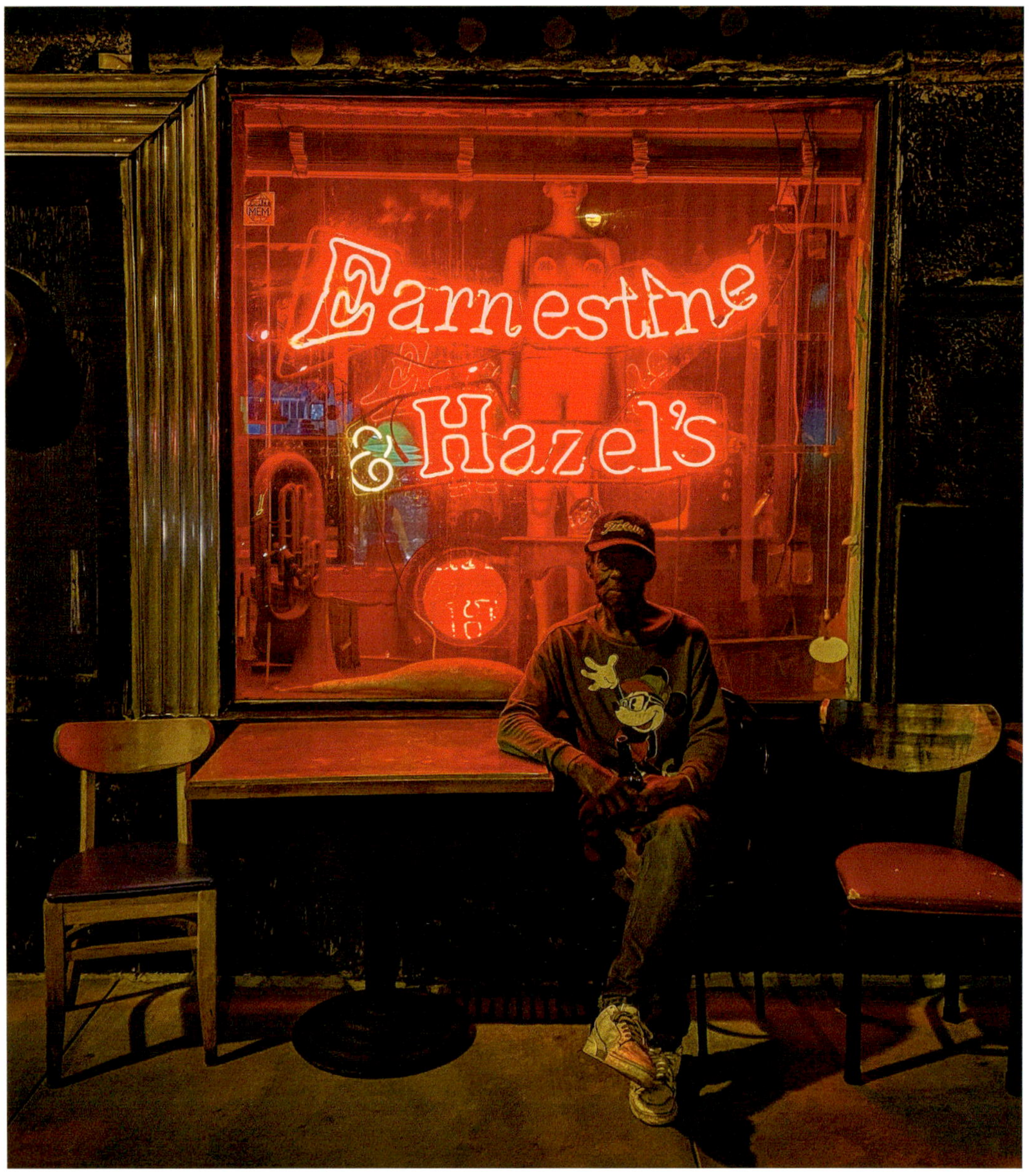

Former brothel, currently haunted, forever serving the delicious Soul Burger. No other dive bar compares to the mighty Earnestine & Hazel's

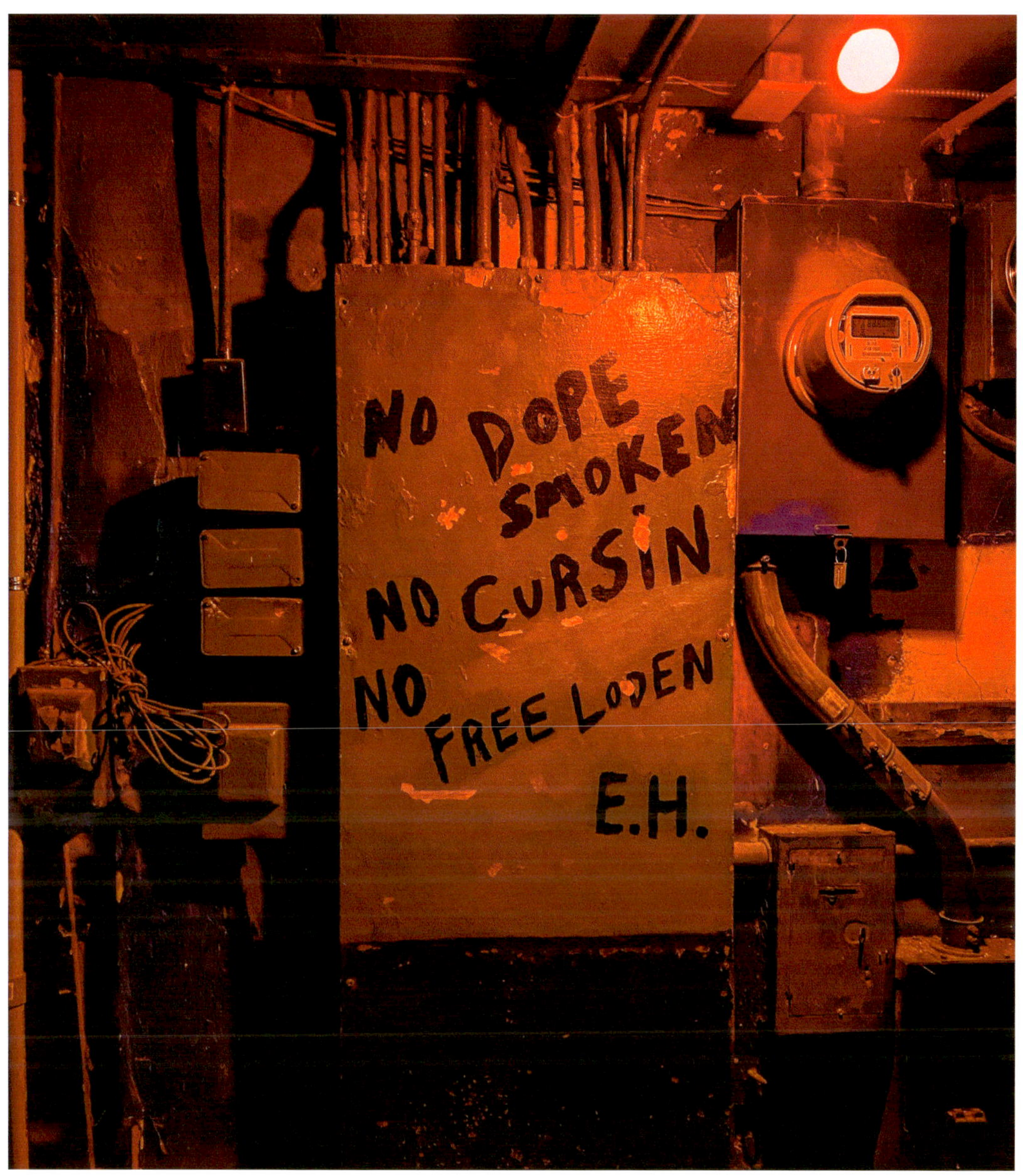

The graffiti at Earnestine & Hazel's is top-notch.

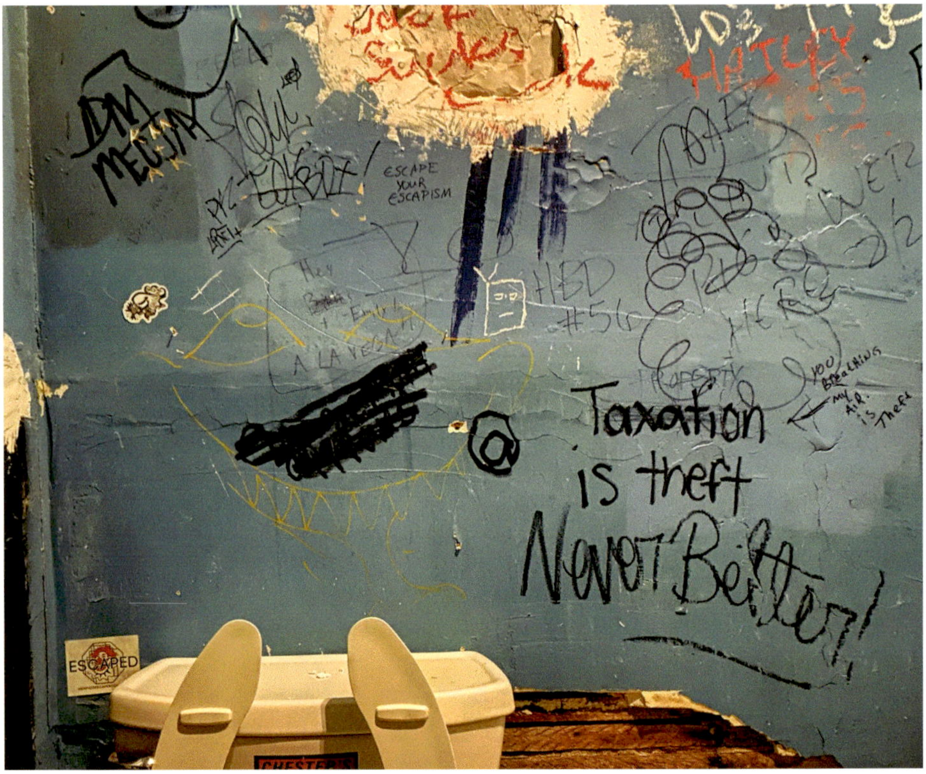

Earnestine & Hazel's: where national and local tax policy is discussed with sophisticated nuance, even in the toilets.

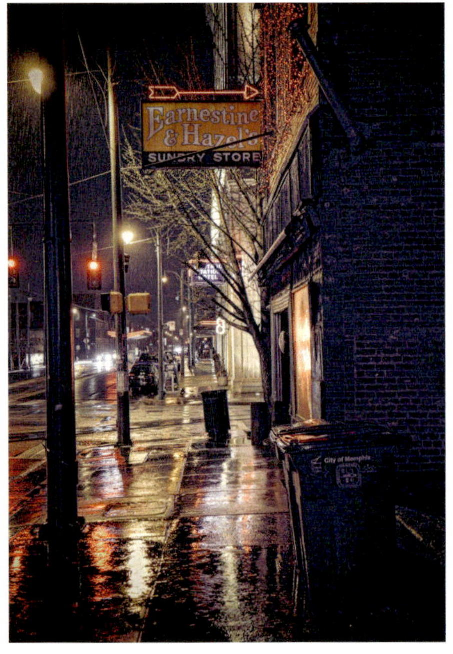

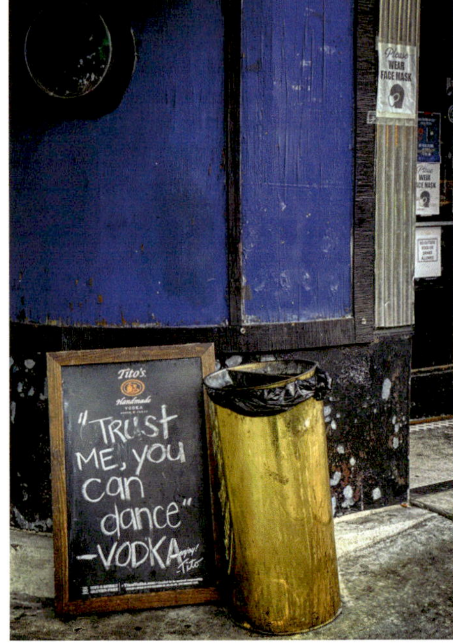

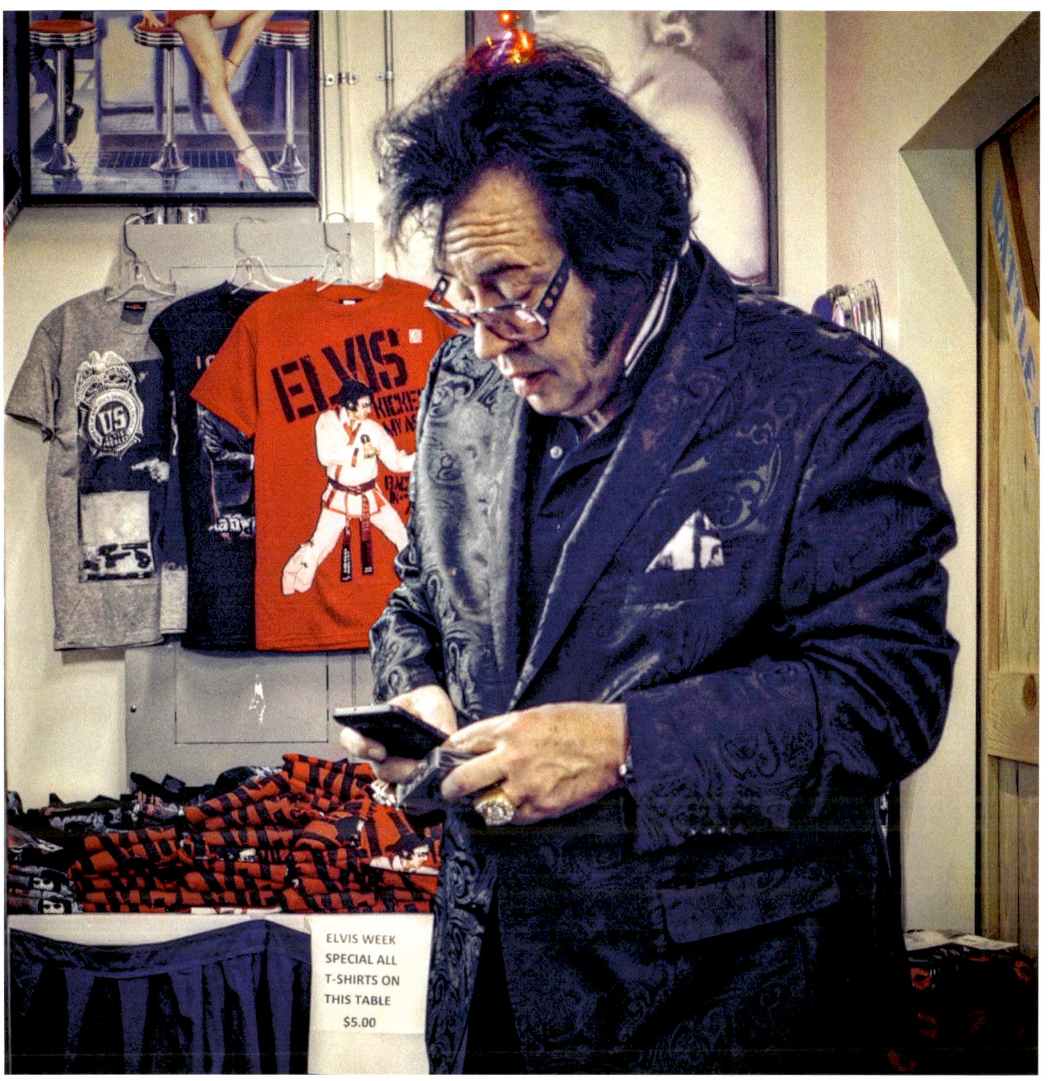

It wouldn't be Memphis without Elvis impersonators. Fun fact: because fewer people tend to travel around Elvis's birthday (January 8), "Elvis Week" is celebrated around the anniversary of his death in mid-August. Locals refer to it as "Death Week".

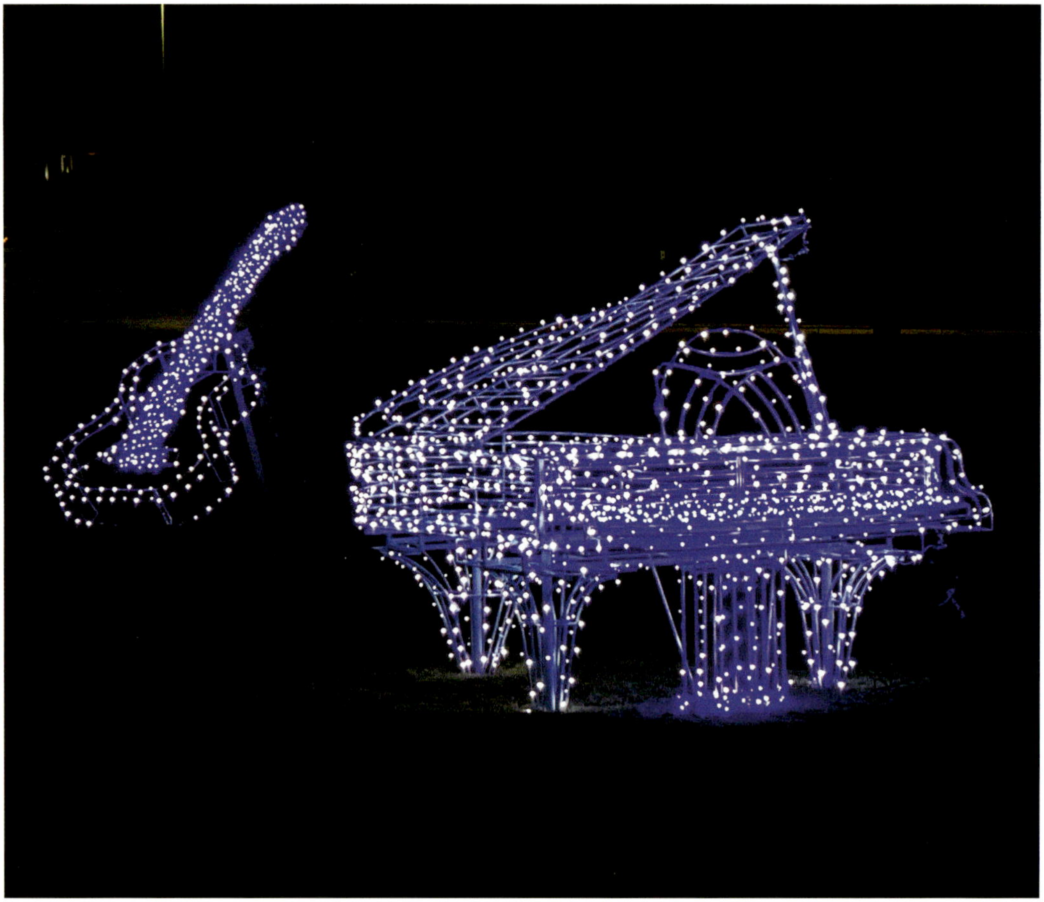

Graceland. Elvis, his parents, and others family members
are buried in the Meditation Garden.

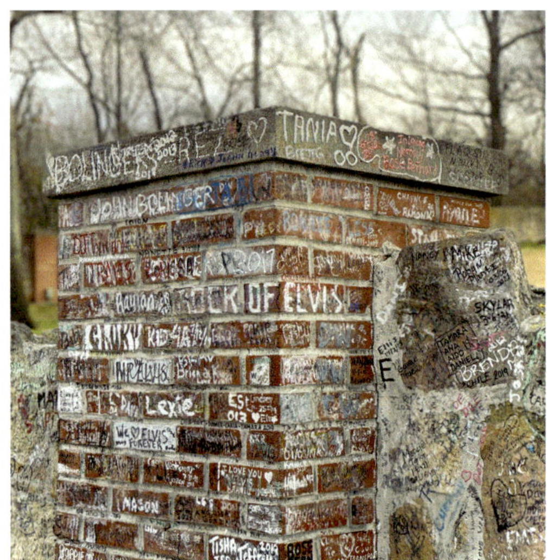

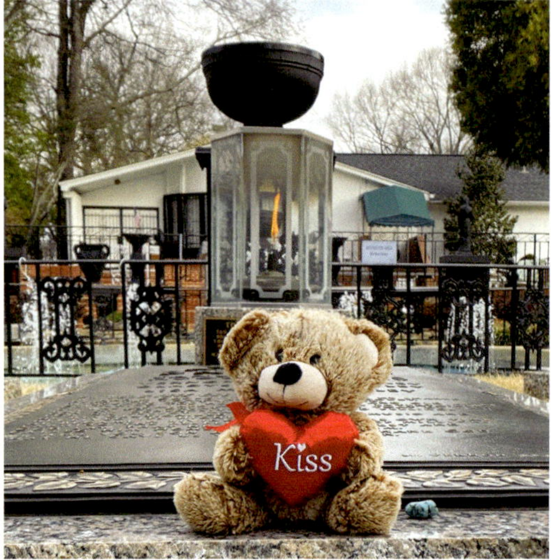

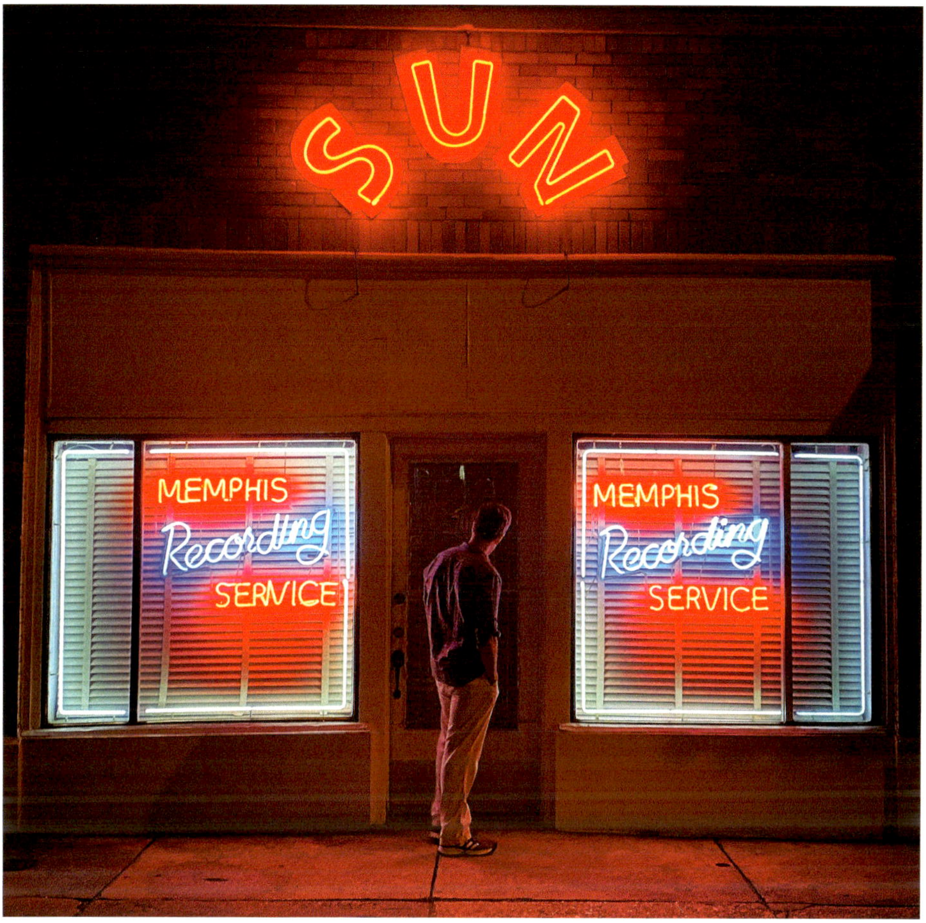

Where rock 'n' roll was born.

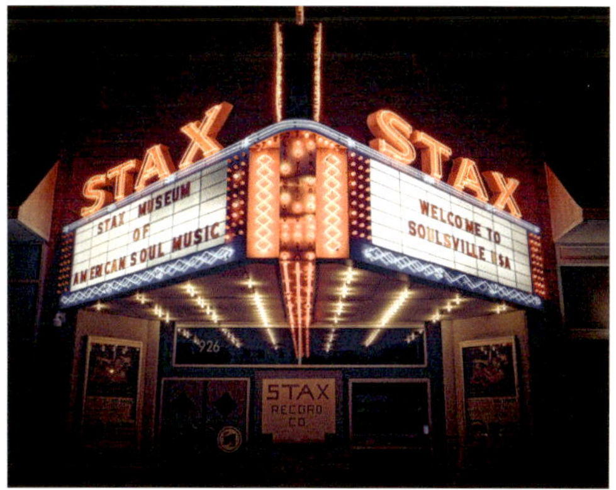

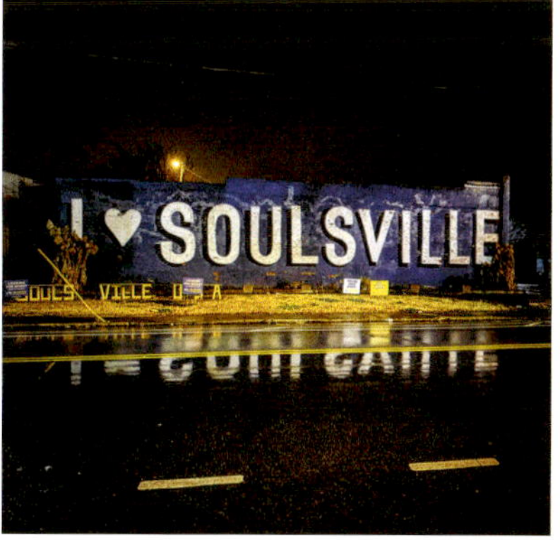

Stax was home to Soul legends like Otis Redding, Isaac Hayes, and the immortal Rufus Thomas.

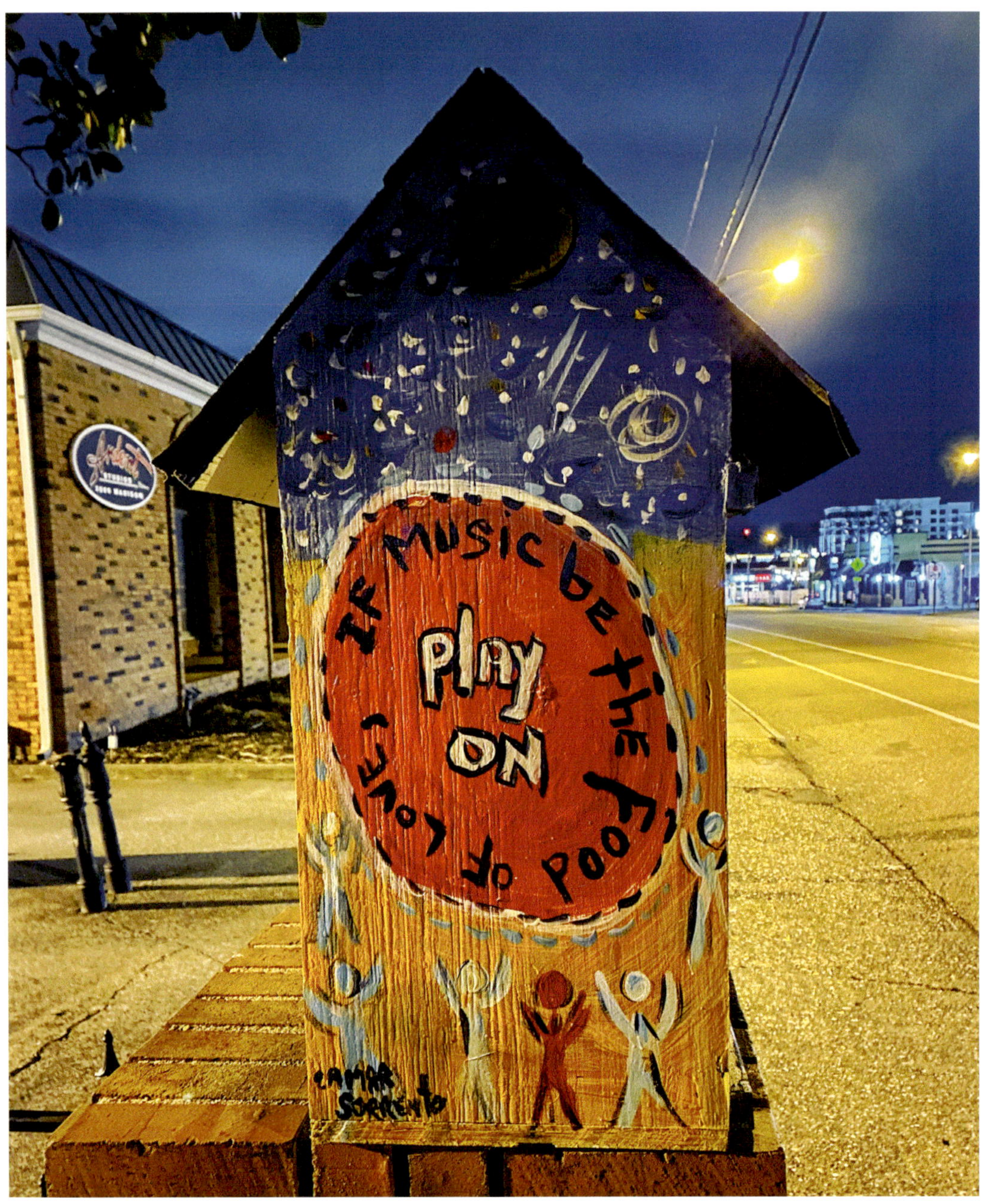

Artists who have recorded or worked at Ardent Studios read like a "who's who" of the music world: Led Zeppelin, Sam and Dave, The Staple Singers, Stevie Ray Vaughan, BB King, The Bar-Kays, The White Stripes, Big Star, Bob Dylan, and many more. The mailbox was painted by local artist Lamar Sorrento and was used to give away complimentary music.

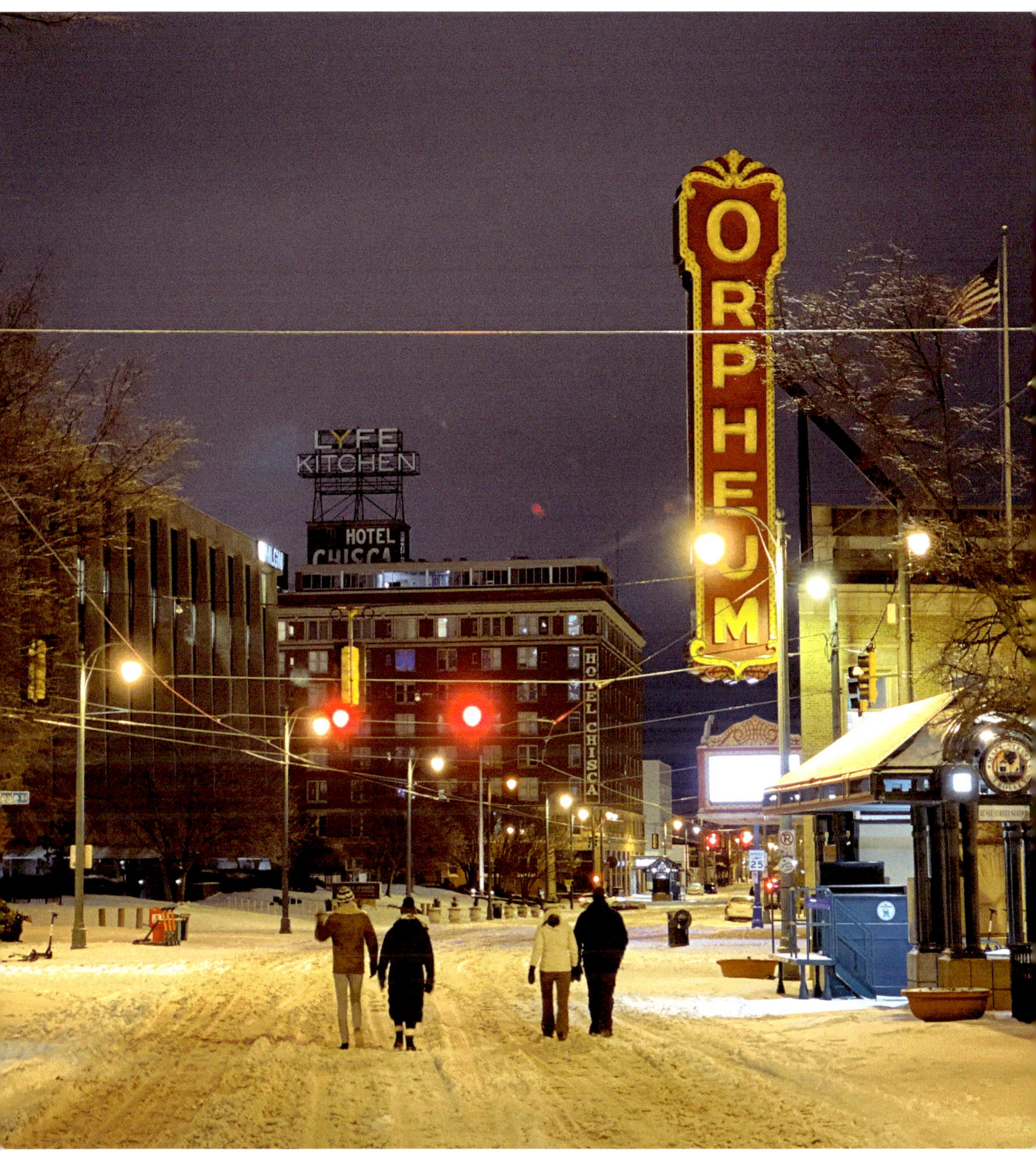

The Orpheum is located on the corner of S Main and Beale. Theater and music acts play there regularly.

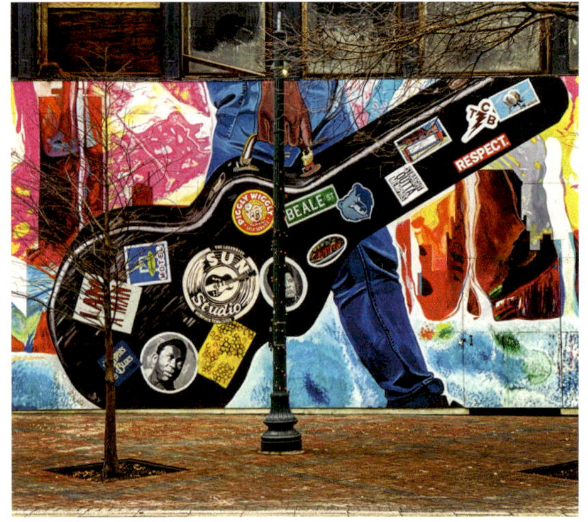

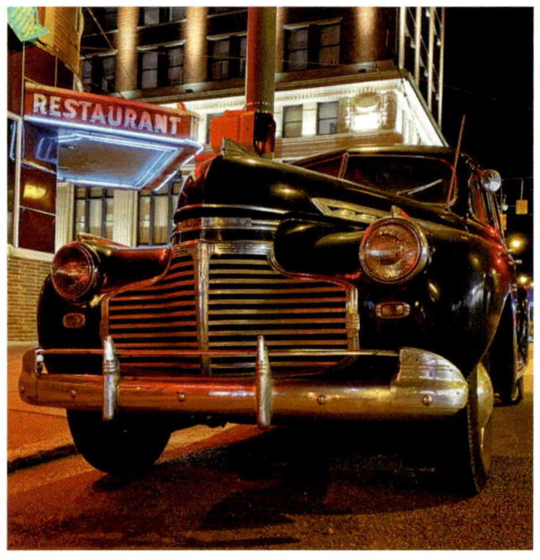

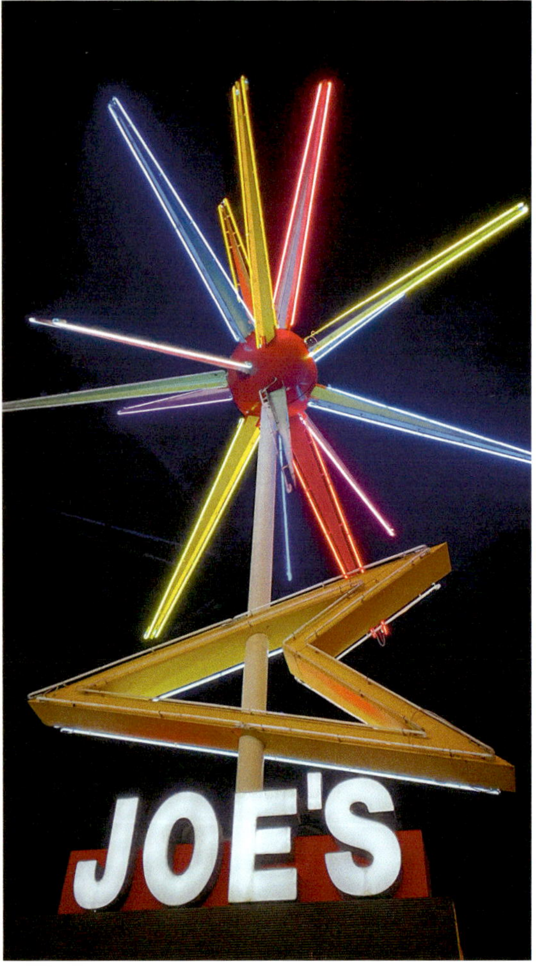

From street signs to a Sputnik adorning a local liquor store, Memphis is replete with artistic expression.

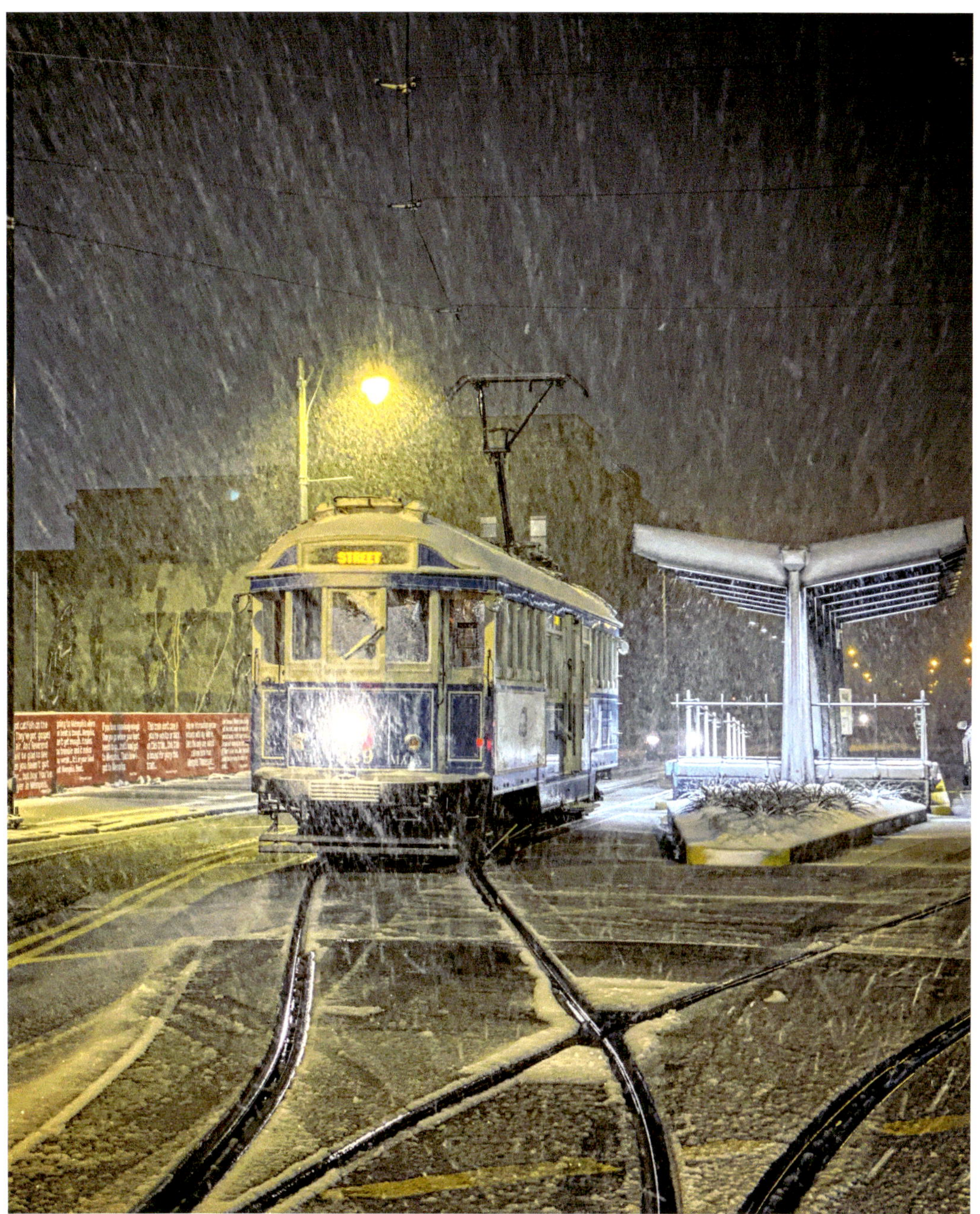

Memphis's trolleys run the length of Main Street. On the last Friday of each month, Trolley Night lets people ride for free and take in all the sights.

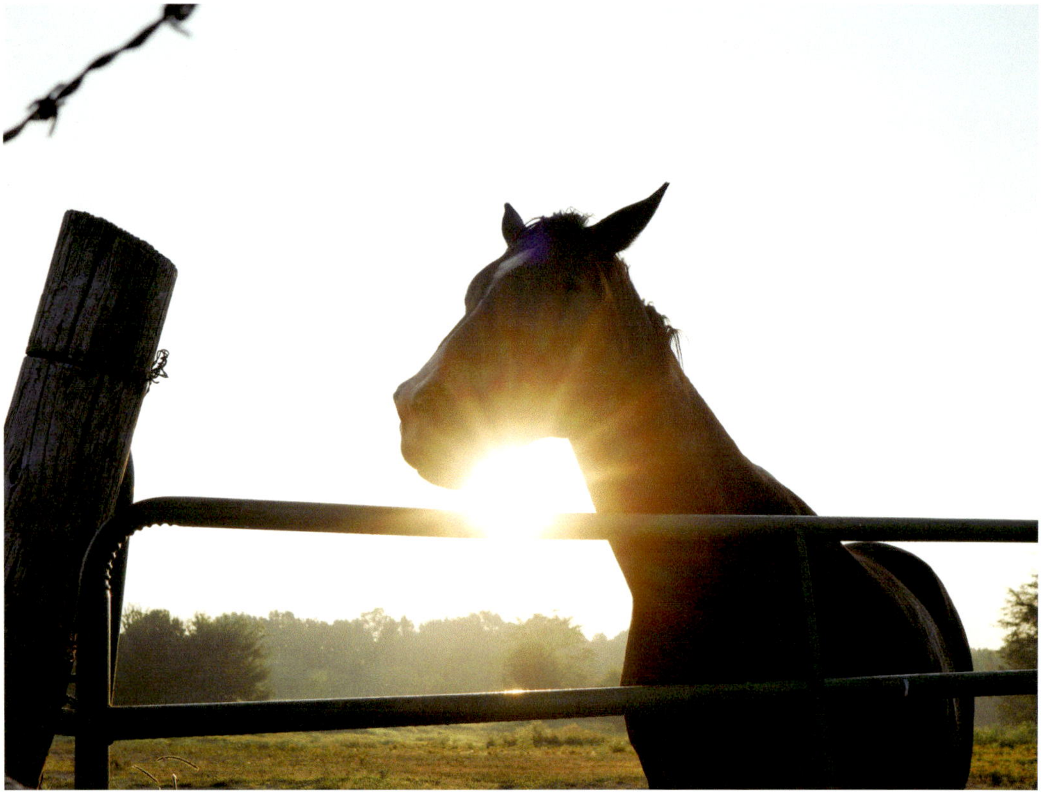

Shelby Farms is filled with nature, beauty, and horses. Seeing the horses run from the stables at daybreak is one of the most beautiful sights you'll ever see.

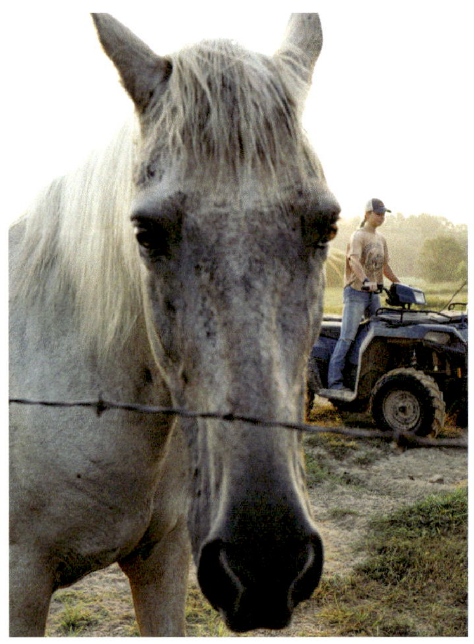

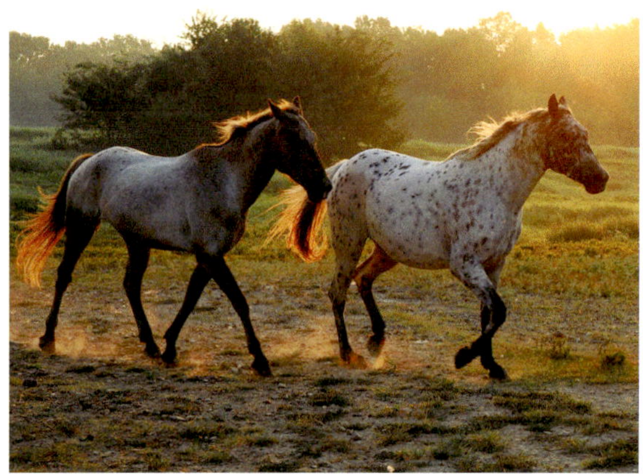

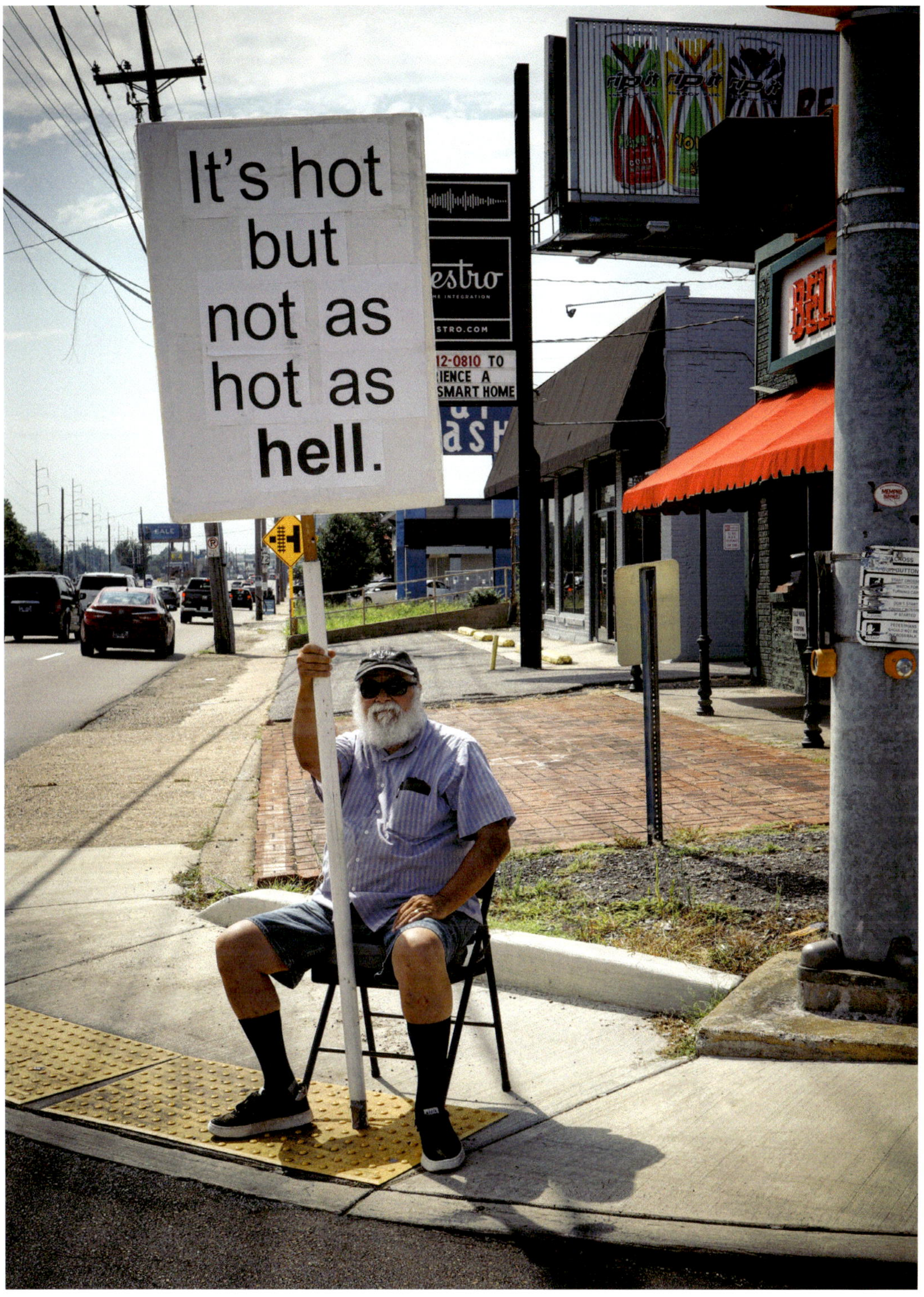

Occasionally, Memphis will remind you that it's in the South.

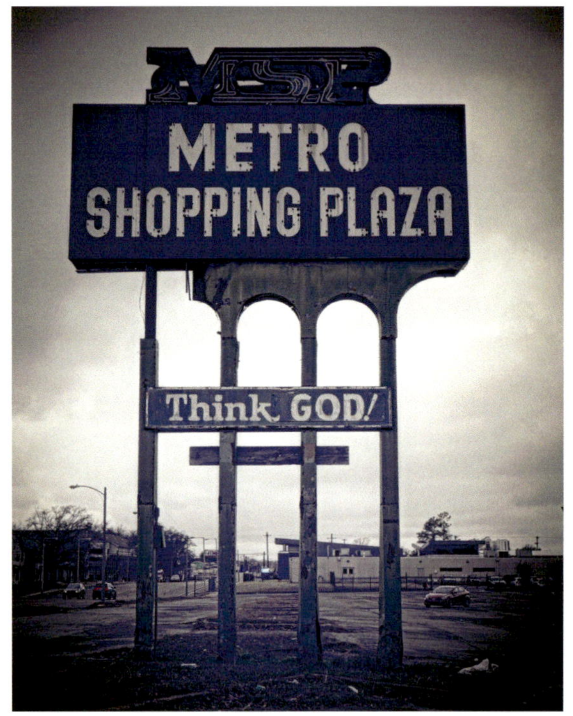
METRO
SHOPPING PLAZA
Think GOD!

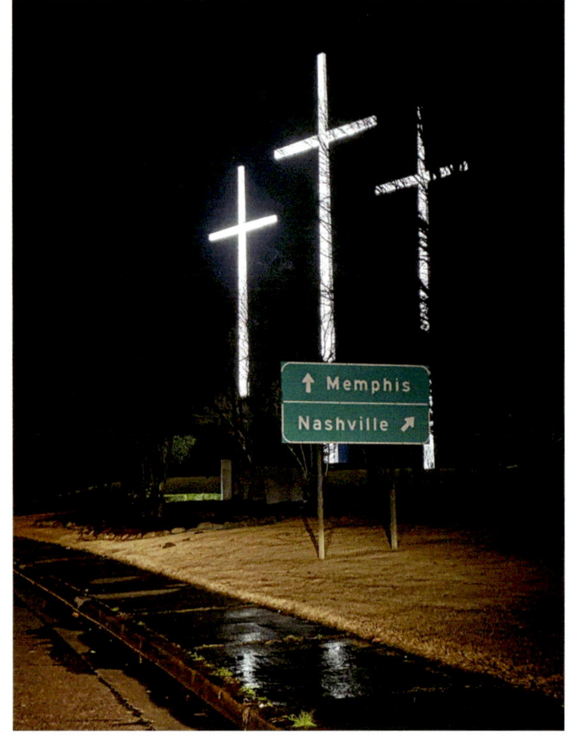
Memphis
Nashville

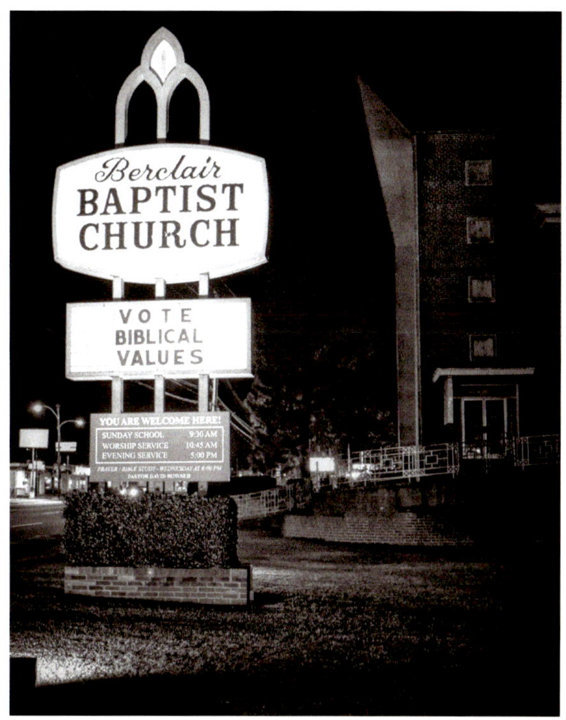
Berclair
BAPTIST
CHURCH
VOTE
BIBLICAL
VALUES
YOU ARE WELCOME HERE!
SUNDAY SCHOOL   9:30 AM
WORSHIP SERVICE   10:45 AM
EVENING SERVICE   5:00 PM
PRAYER / BIBLE STUDY - WEDNESDAY AT 6:00 PM
PASTOR DAVID MOSSER

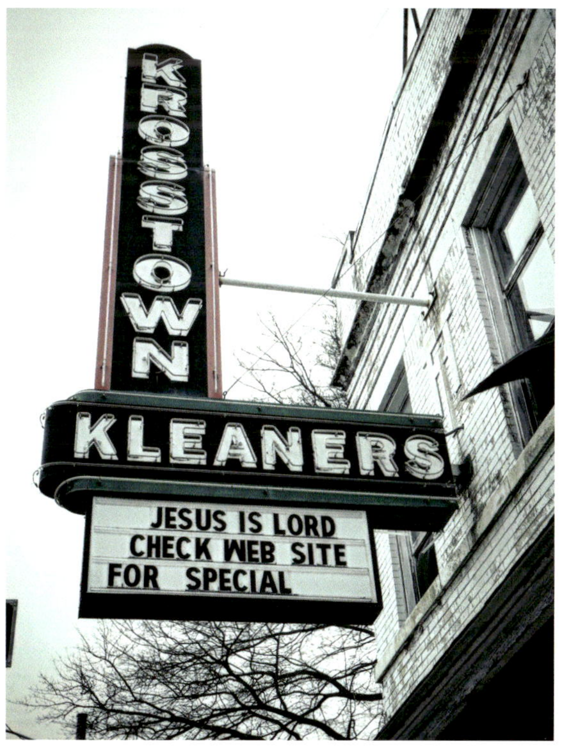
KROSSTOWN
KLEANERS
JESUS IS LORD
CHECK WEB SITE
FOR SPECIAL

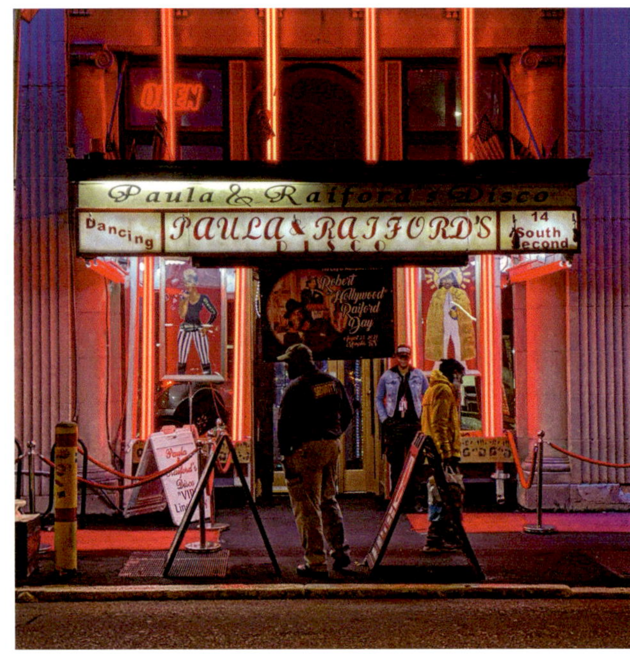

Paula & Raiford's is a famous downtown dance club. The place is packed on weekends, but everyone still finds enough room to dance.

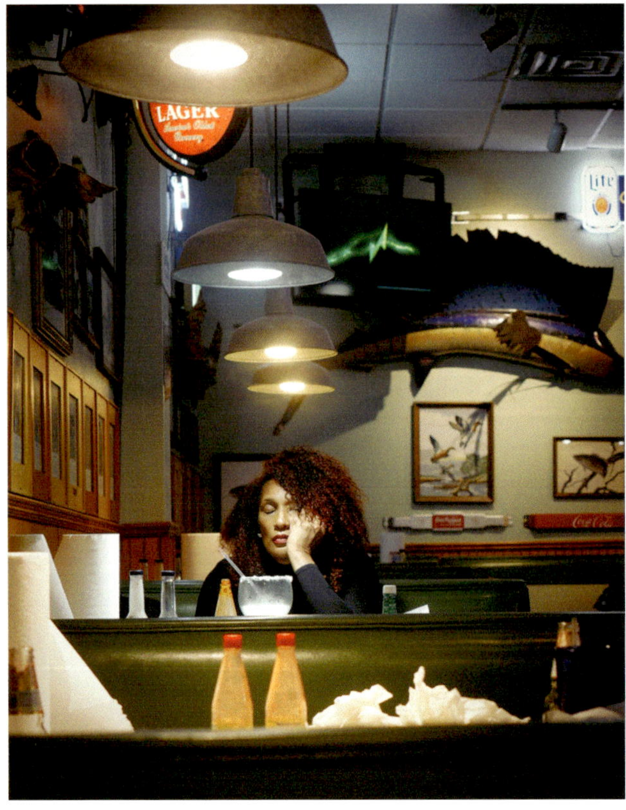

Even Memphians sometimes are just SO over it.

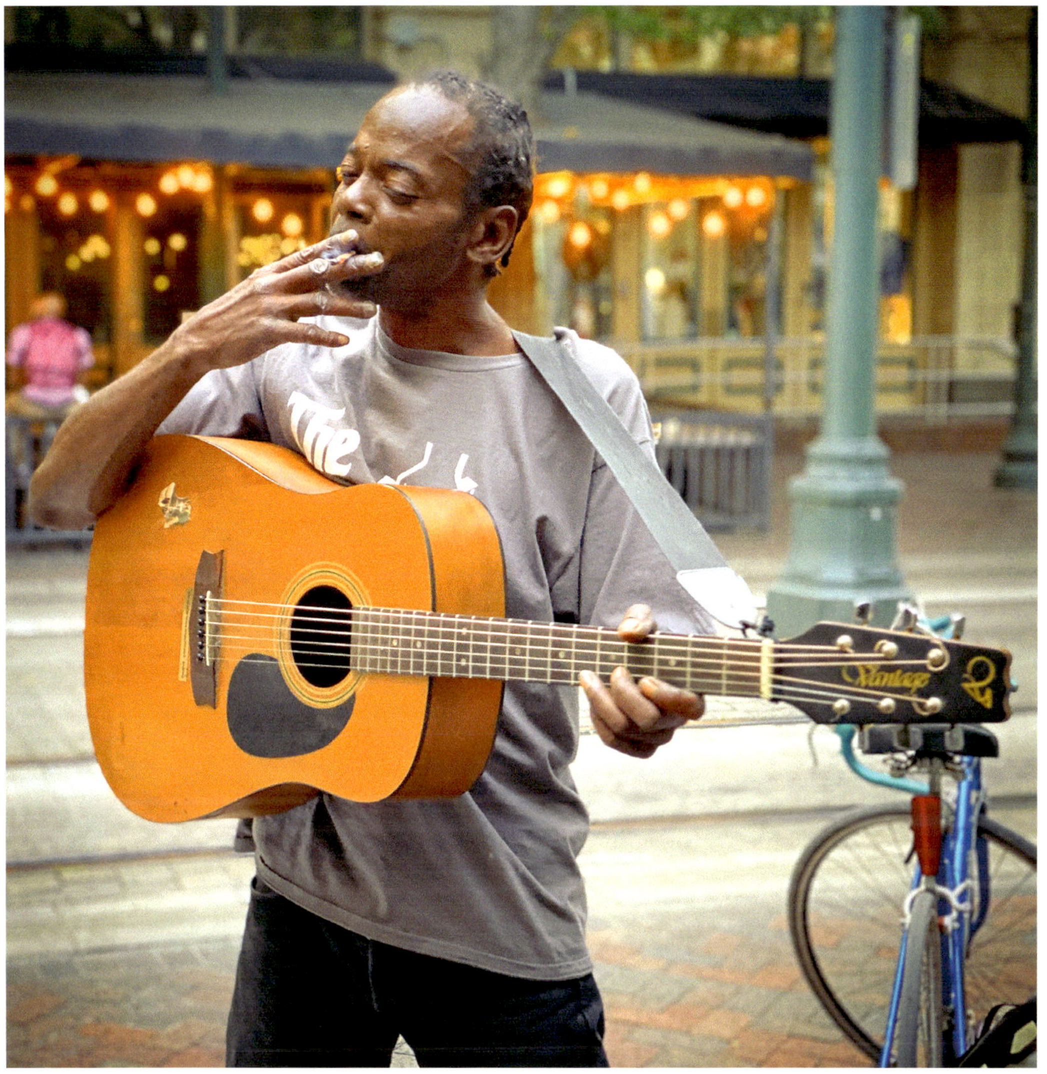

Street musicians can be found throughout downtown.

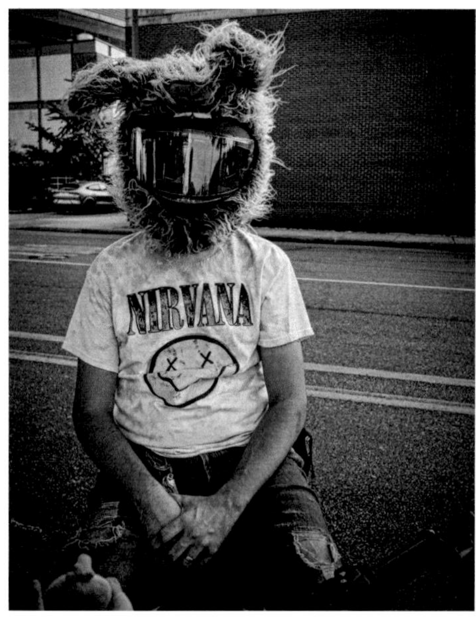

From downtown grunge to uptown class, Memphis has it all.

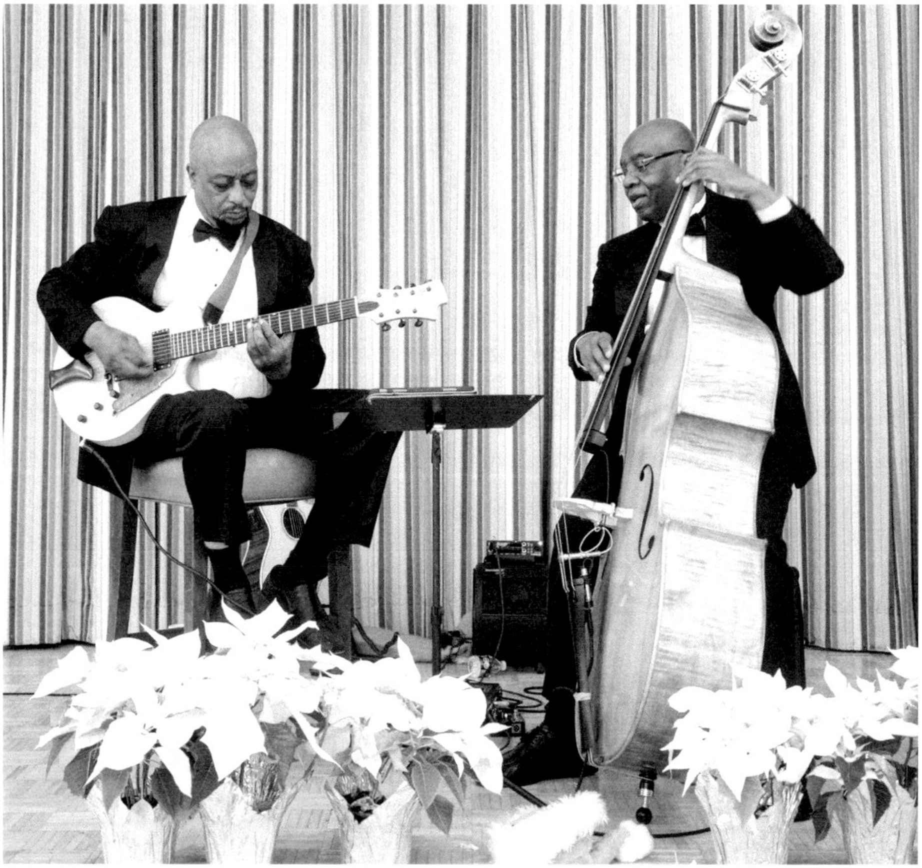

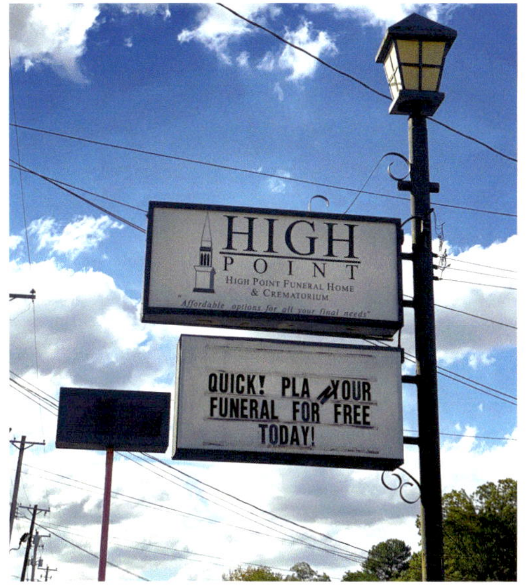

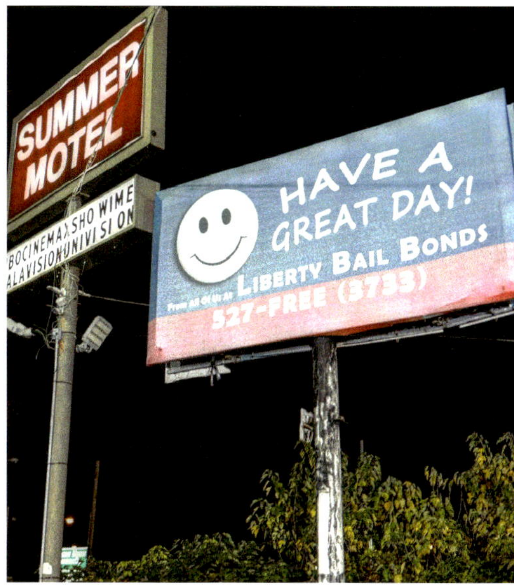

Sometimes I can't tell if Memphis intends all its humor, but I'll take it one way or the other.

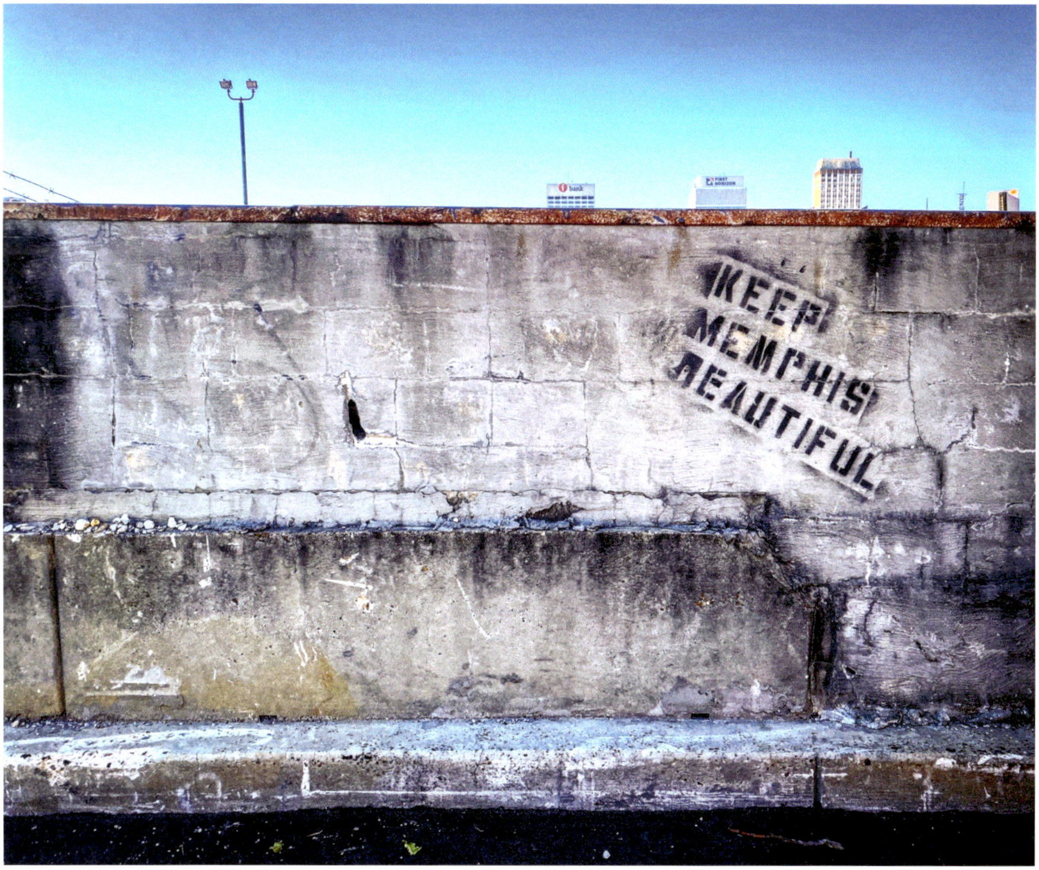

3

Civil Rights

On my first trip to Memphis, I visited Clarksdale, Mississippi (the subject of the next chapter). I wound up having a long conversation with a local. Eventually, he asked where I was staying. When I said I was staying up in Memphis, he was taken aback and asked what it was like.

"A little weird," I told him, "All the restaurants were closed by 9pm."

"Yeah," he answered. "That's probably because the staff don't want to get killed in a drive-by."

He wasn't joking. Memphis has a long-standing issue with crime and gang-related violence. It has one of the highest poverty rates in the nation, an abundance of substandard housing, and a severe problem with education. In a study released in 2020, Memphis ranked #468 out of 511 cities for educational attainment.

Today, billboards have headlines like "Real Men Don't Murder." Memphis consistently ranks in America's Top Ten Most Dangerous Cities. And the trouble seems to be accelerating.

But this is nothing new for Memphis. This is, after all, where Martin Luther King Jr. was tragically shot to death in 1968 by a racist escaped convict.

The problems of Memphis are directly tied to the nation's centuries-old battle for civil rights. The city's ethnic breakdown is nearly two-thirds African American, but only in 2021 was a statue of Confederate States of America Lt. General and first-era Ku Klux Klan Grand Wizard Nathan Bedford Forrest wearing a Confederate States of America uniform finally removed from public city grounds. The problems in education mean there is little upward mobility for all too many of the city's youth. The cycle of poverty continues.

For many, the way out of poverty seems to become part of a gang. Memphis's gun-related violence has become a national issue. In 2023, more than 160 children between the ages of nine and fourteen were hospitalized after being shot—a new record.

For me, the gun violence was brought closer than ever on April 30, 2023. It was the Sunday afternoon to kick off the Memphis in May festivities. Some friends and

I went to Beale Street to watch the wine racing event. Soon after the challenge began, we heard gunfire. An altercation between a vendor nicknamed Bubbles and a passerby resulted in the latter firing his gun at Bubbles. The bullet fortunately only grazed Bubbles' head but hit a waiter in the hand who was across the street—a blue-skied Sunday afternoon on Memphis's most populated streets suddenly turned tragic, wounding two. After that, I learned to be more careful and always be aware of my surroundings.

One thing was immediately apparent as the shooter lay on the ground after being zip-tied by a local security guard and they waited for the police. The man was strangely proud. He had proven his toughness by firing his gun on a crowded street. His girlfriend defiantly defended him, and he had a bizarre serenity on his face. Why? My only conclusion is that perhaps he had legitimated himself amongst his peers. And issues like this always correlate with civil rights.

The city's civil rights troubles rose in another way in 2023 in the wake of the senseless and brutal murder of Tyre Nichols. Nichols was a twenty-nine-year-old African American man passionate about photography and skateboarding. On the night of January 7, he was pulled over by members of the Memphis Police Department Scorpion Unit. In the video footage that surfaced in the aftermath, the officers pulled Nichols from his car and then pepper sprayed and tasered him. Nichols ran away, but the officers caught up with him. Without apparent cause, they proceeded to beat him mercilessly. When medics arrived, they failed to administer care for nearly twenty minutes. Nichols was admitted to the hospital in critical condition. He never regained consciousness and died of his injuries on January 10.

The video footage shocked the city and the world. Less than three years after George Floyd's death, Memphis prepared for potential riots and violence. The fact that most of the officers involved in the violence were also African American did little to alleviate the tension or ill will.

But then Memphis did something that seemed to surprise everyone … except Memphis. There were numerous protests on the streets, in City Hall, and on social media, but there was no violence. Everyone seemed united in asking how to improve the city and ensure this never happens again.

For me, it displayed Memphis at its best. There was anger but not rage, emotion but also rational probing and a search for answers and solutions to the underlying problems. Like civil rights champion Martin Luther King Jr., who was gunned down in front of his room at the Lorraine Hotel, and the city eventually transformed the site into the remarkable National Civil Rights Museum, Memphis turned tragedy into something meaningful.

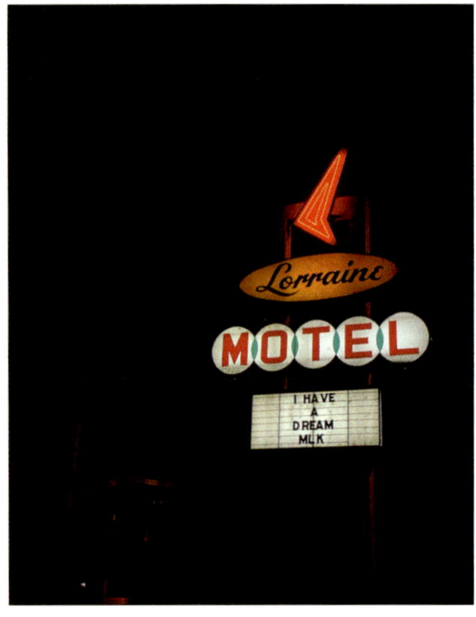

Left: The National Civil Rights Museum, formally the Lorraine Hotel, where Martin Luther King, Jr. was killed on April 4, 1968.

Below: MLK's room.

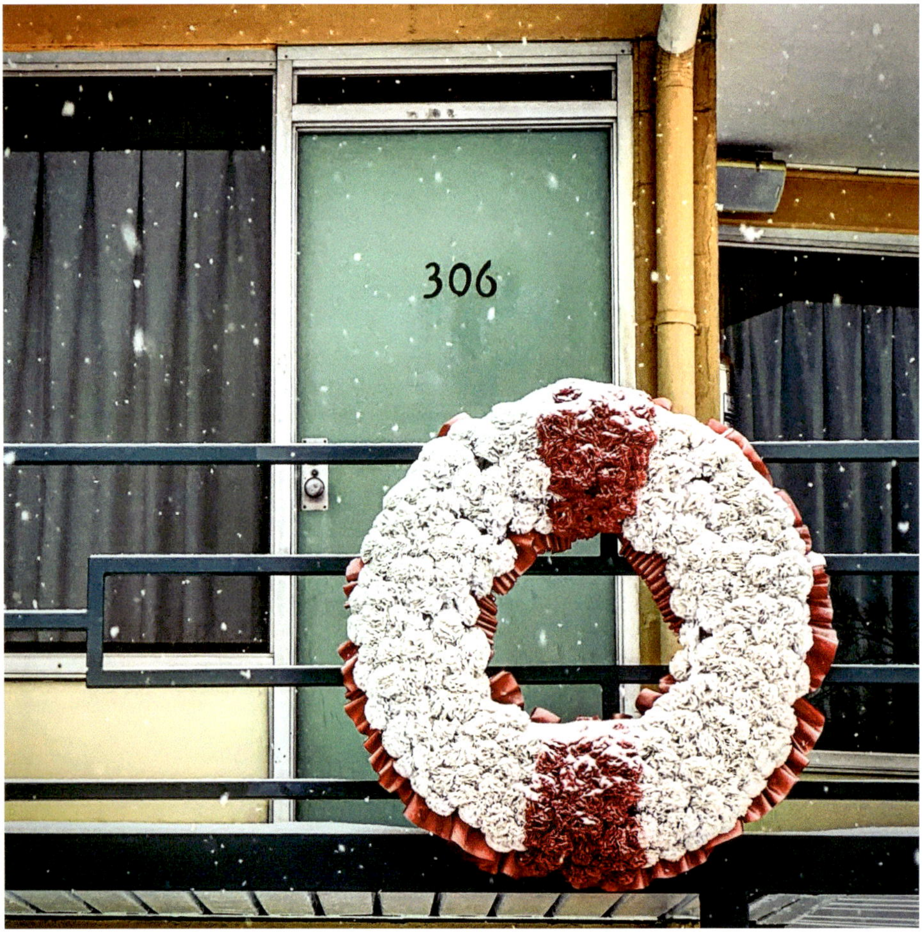

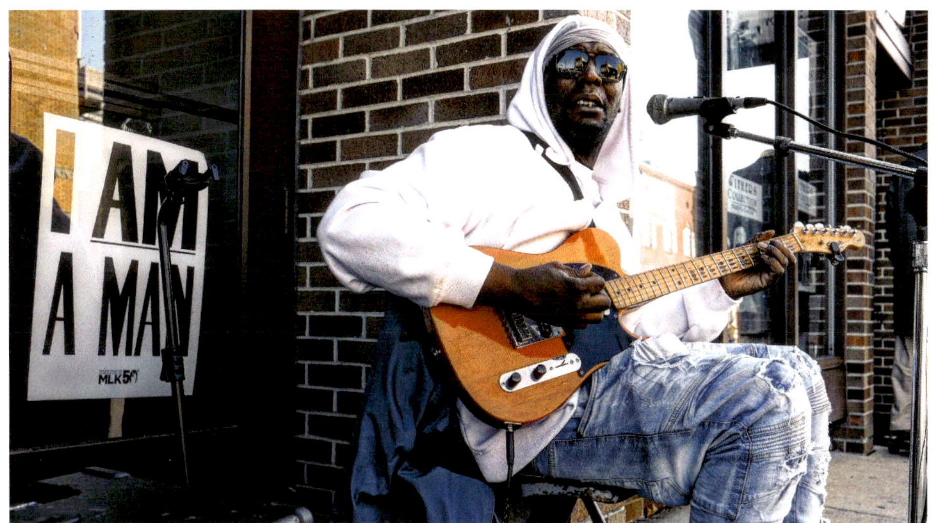

MLK was in Memphis that day to help lead a strike by the local sanitation workers, promoting safer and better working conditions. The phrase "I Am a Man" was their slogan.

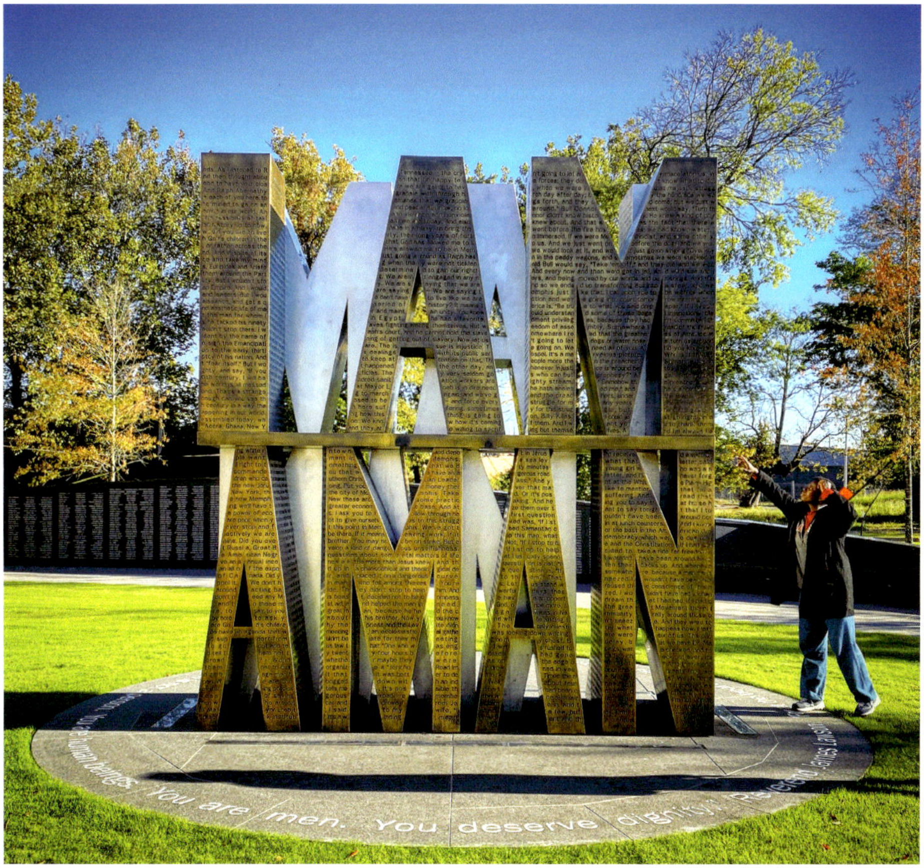

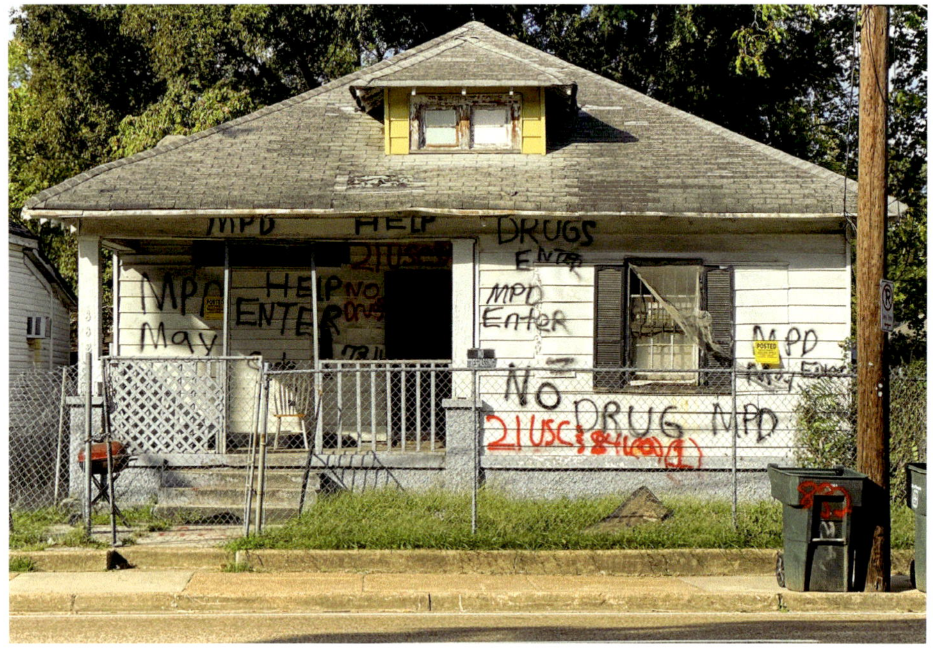

Shortfalls in educational funding have caused far too many Memphians to be illiterate. That signage like this can be found all too frequently is tragic.

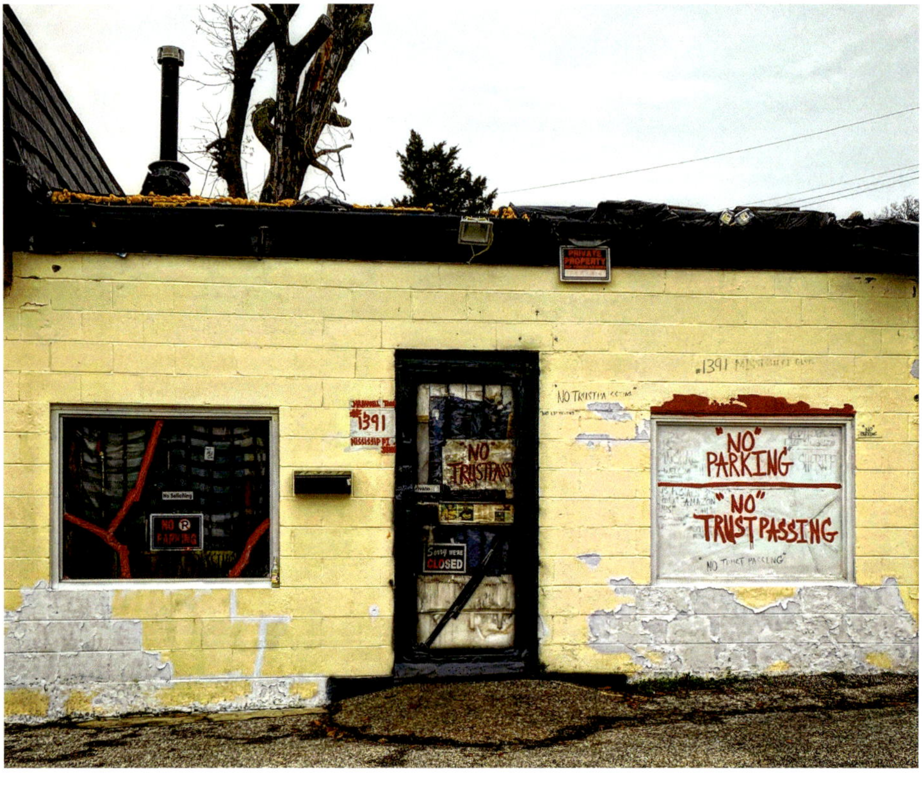

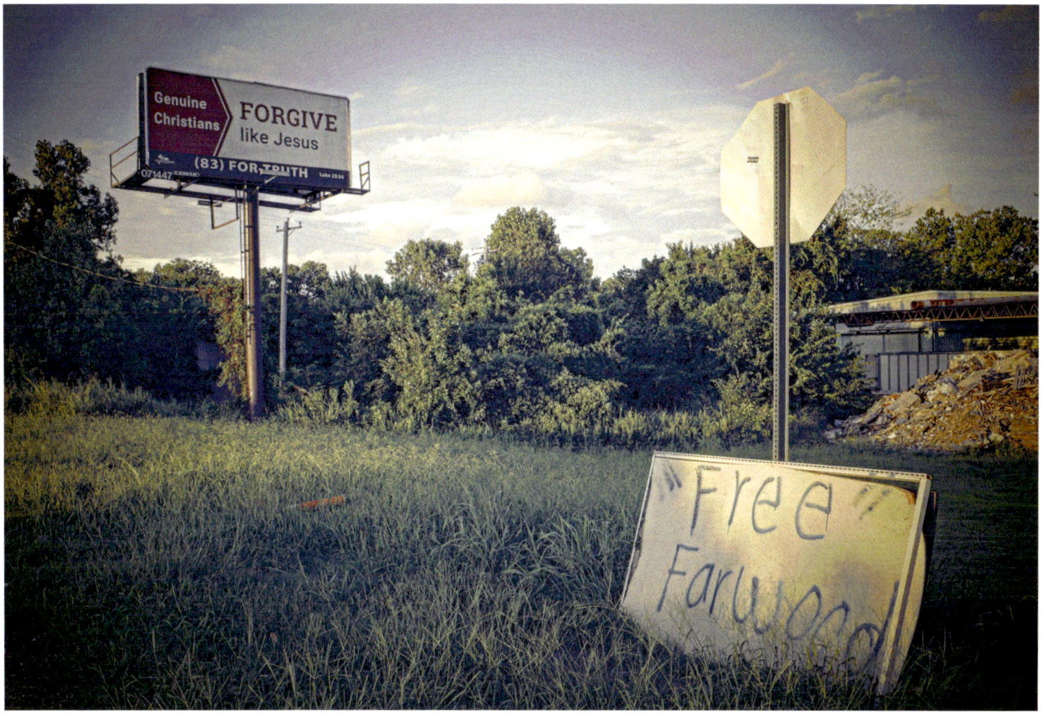

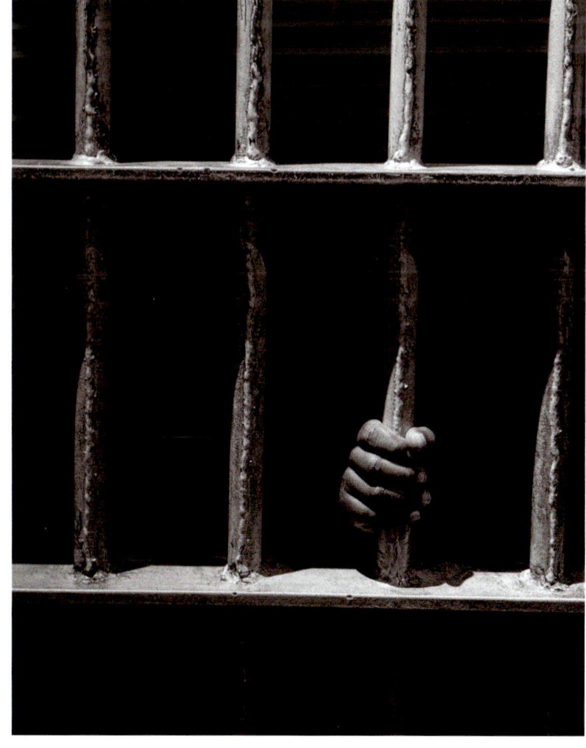

Right: A child explores the demonstration prison cell inside the National Civil Rights Museum.

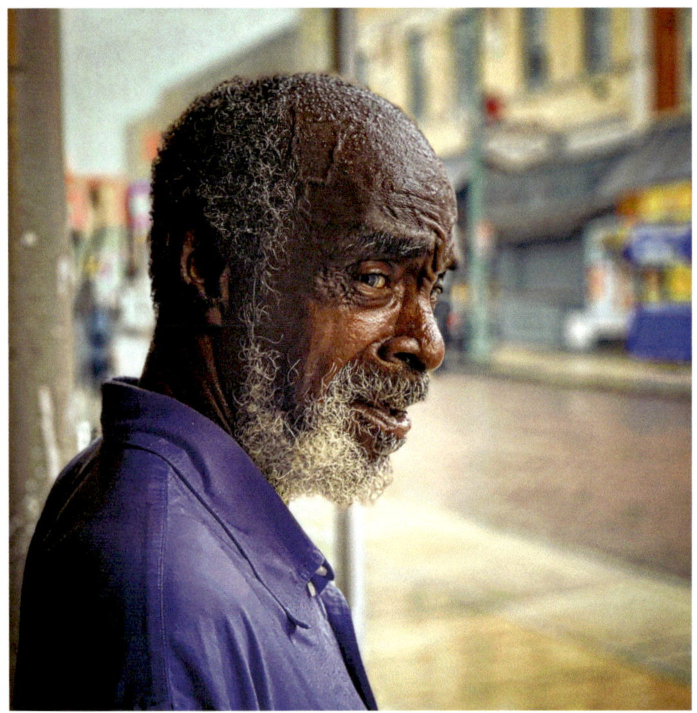

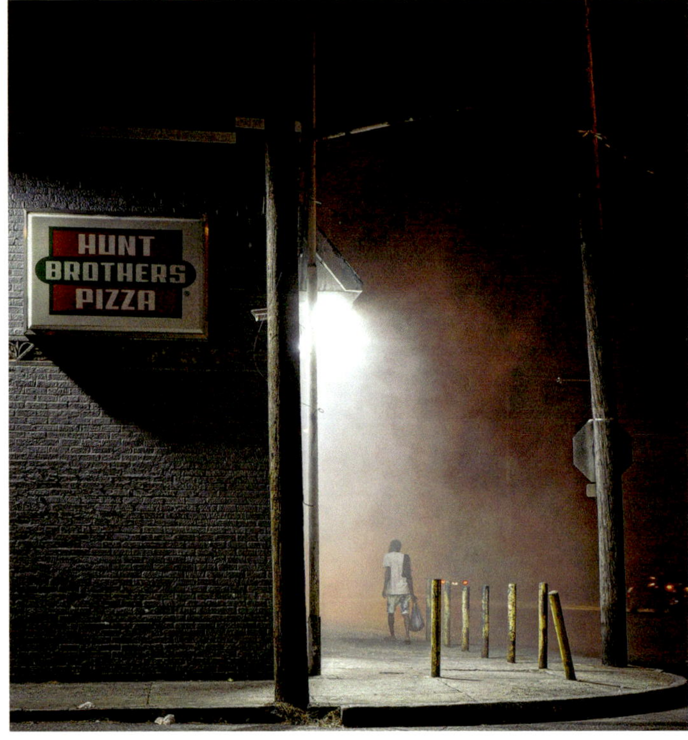

It's not that the War on Poverty was lost; it's that it hasn't been won YET.

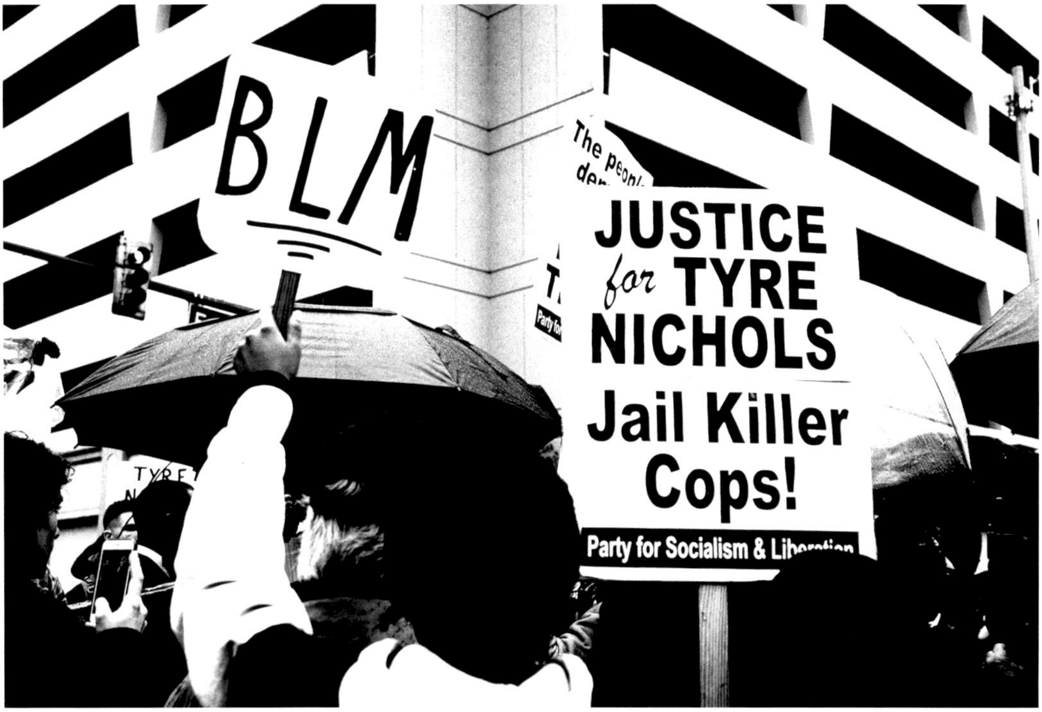

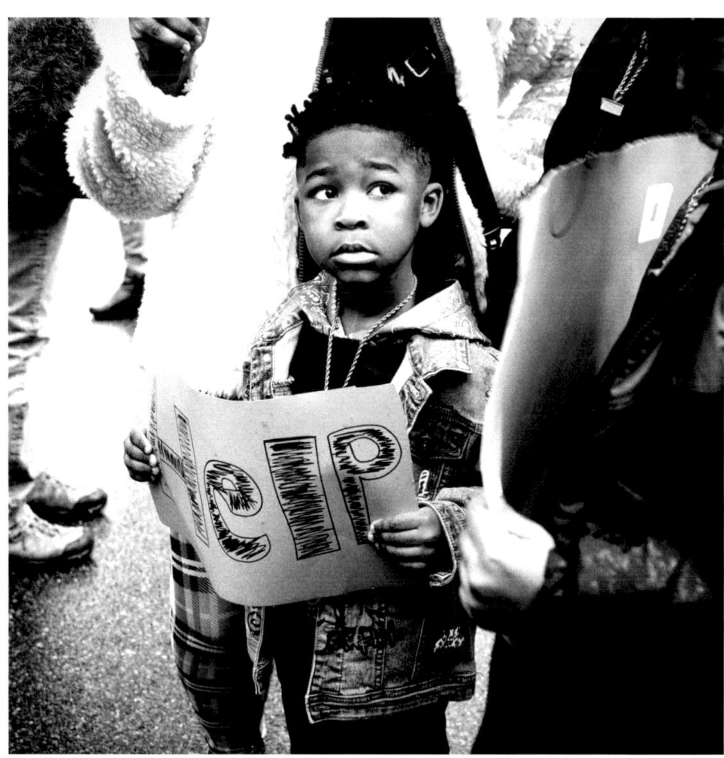

Above: A protest march for Tyre Nichols.

Right: A child holds up a poignant sign at the march.

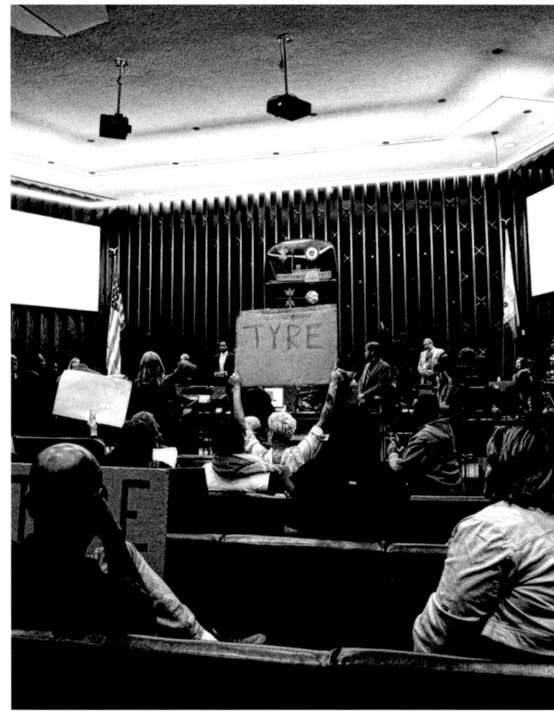

Protesters attended City Hall meetings in frustration that Memphis continued to conduct business as usual in the wake of Nichols' death.

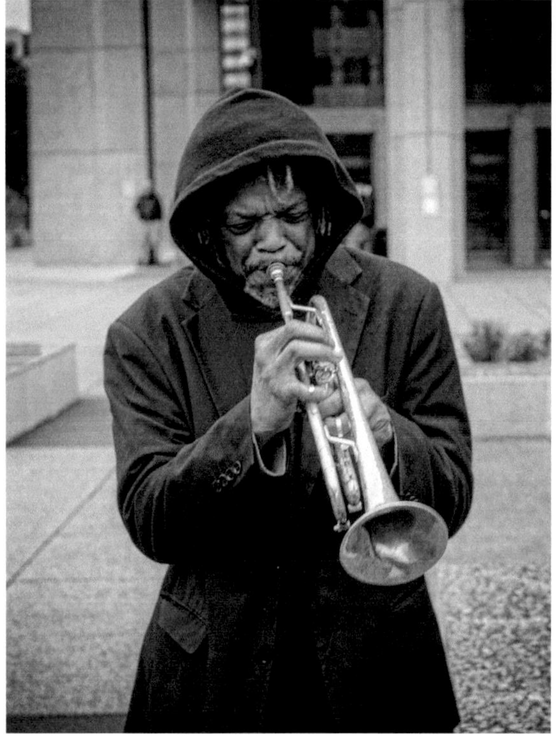

Playing taps at the close of the protest march.

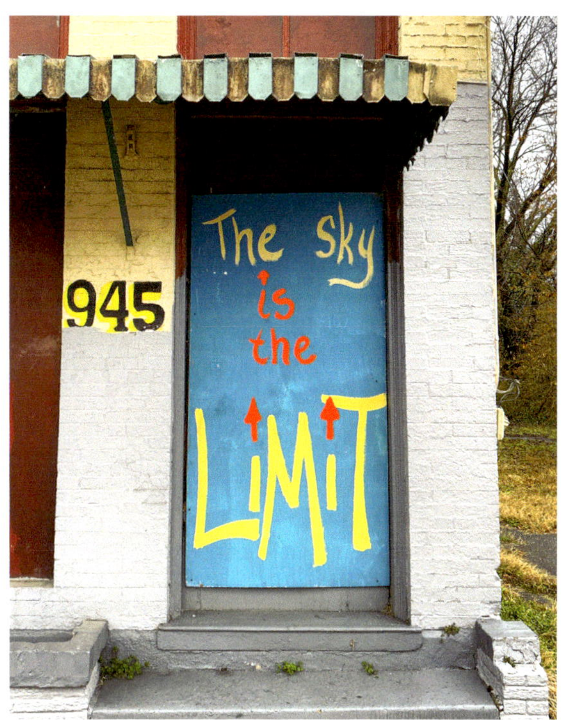

Children's art at McLemore Avenue.

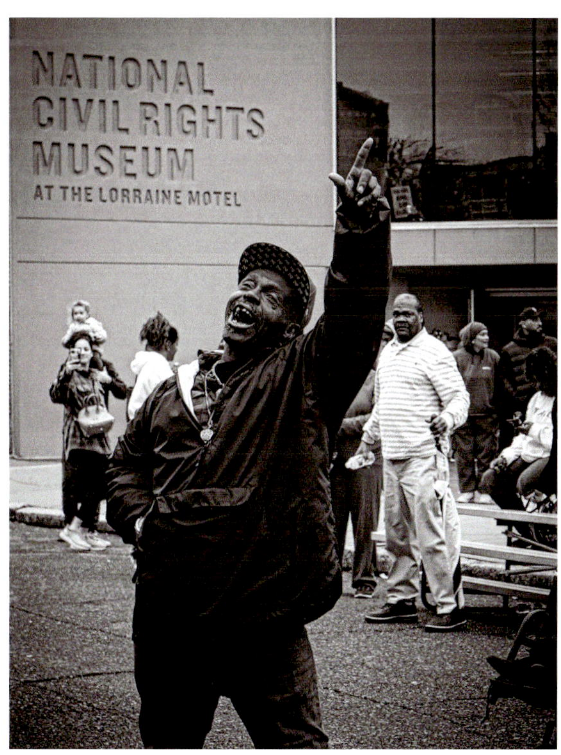

Celebrations on MLK Day at the
National Civil Rights Museum.

4

Clarksdale

So why is a book about Memphis taking a detour into the Mississippi Delta? If you know and care about the Blues, then you know places like Clarksdale are an essential part of Memphis's story.

Several towns in Mississippi played a crucial role in how the blues came to Memphis. B.B. King was from outside of Itta Bena. The Tutwiler train station is where W. C. Handy awoke from a nap and heard a man playing slide guitar with a knife, resulting in "the strangest music" he ever heard. Arguably the most important of all is the area around Clarksdale, where music legends Muddy Waters, John Lee Hooker, Sam Cooke, and others are from. But that's not all: Clarksdale is also where the greatest fable of the blues originates: The Legend of the Crossroads.

The story goes that Robert Johnson, a young, aspiring musician, went to the Crossroads late at night and made a deal with the Devil. In exchange for his immortal soul, Satan bestowed upon Johnson great musical talent and popularity. You could argue the Devil upheld his side of the bargain because Johnson's music and guitar playing are still renowned by musicians and blues fans. Songs like "Crossroad Blues," "Me and the Devil Blues," "Hellhound on My Trail," and more all conveyed the desperation and fear of a man being pursued by the hosts of Hell. Johnson died at the age of twenty-seven, purportedly poisoned by a jealous bartender because Johnson was hitting on the bartender's wife. But his music lives on, with famous cover versions of his songs by The Rolling Stones, Eric Clapton, Led Zeppelin, and more.

The first time I visited Clarksdale, I found myself in a conversation with a local. Eventually, I asked about the location of the Crossroads. He looked at his watch and said, "I ain't got nothing going on. C'mon, I'll take you."

We can debate the wisdom of getting into a car with a stranger in rural Mississippi at another time. The important thing is I hopped in. As he drove along, he'd point at a location. "Now, some people think the Crossroads was here," and he'd point at the local train station. "And others think it was *here*," and he'd point towards a local cemetery. "Me? I personally think it was here," he said as we drove past some nondescript road. "But the one thing I can tell you for certain?" He stopped the car in the parking lot of Abe's BBQ and pointed upwards. "It was NOT here." Sure enough, we were at the crossing of Highways 61 and 49, where the city erected a landmark of three electric guitars marking the supposed site of the Crossroads.

Regardless of where the Crossroads is, Clarksdale's importance in the history of American music and Delta Blues is beyond question. By the 1950s, musicians were traveling to Memphis to be part of the big music scene on Beale Street and to record in the city. One example is Jackie Brenston and his Delta Cats, featuring Ike Turner on piano. The band was traveling from Clarksdale to Memphis when the guitar amp they strapped to the top of their car came loose and crashed onto the highway. When they arrived at Memphis Recording Service (soon to become Sun Records), they were distraught because the amp's tubes and sound were audibly damaged. But studio owner Sam Phillips was delighted. The distorted crunch that the amp now created was unique, exciting, and innovative. As a result, the record, called "Rocket 88," is now hailed as the very first Rock & Roll record.

If you visit Memphis, the 70-mile trip to Clarksdale should be part of your itinerary. The drive along Highway 61 is interesting enough: you'll drive through the casino town Tunica, long stretches of cotton fields, and more. But Clarksdale itself is the destination. Rock out at Ground Zero Blues Club (co-owned by Clarksdale native Morgan Freeman, who frequently is in attendance!), Red's Blues Club, one of the last Juke Joints still standing, and the Shack Up Inn, built on an old plantation and featuring some of the funkiest, most eccentric architecture in the world.

Every April, Clarksdale hosts the annual Juke Joint Festival, bringing music lovers from all over the world into the tiny town. And the best part? Clarksdale is doing more than just trading on some long-lost past. Contemporary locals like Christone "Kingfish" Ingram, Anthony "Big A" Sherrod, and others are taking the blues into exciting new directions and continue to expand the music and its possibilities for the twenty-first century.

When music is this good, you do have to debate whether selling your immortal soul is worth it!

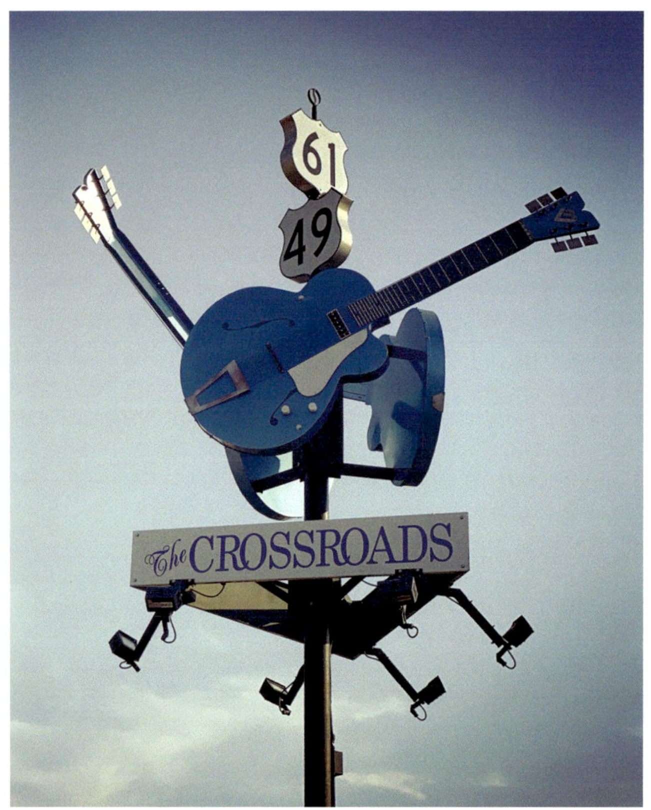

Left: At the Crossroads of Highways 49 and 61.

Below: Blues Alley in Clarksdale, MS.

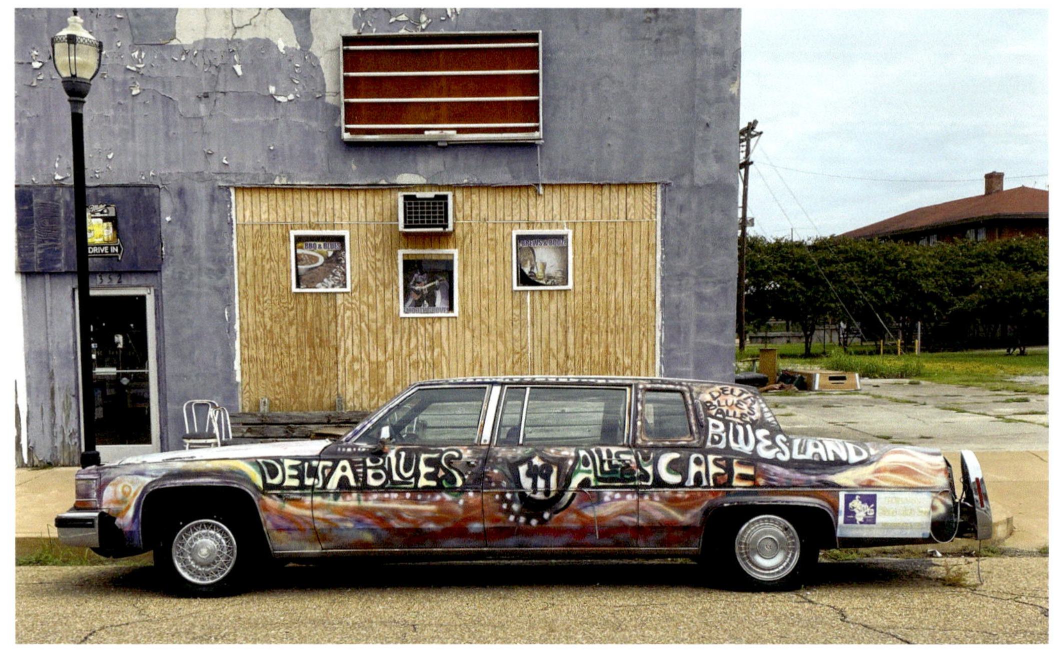

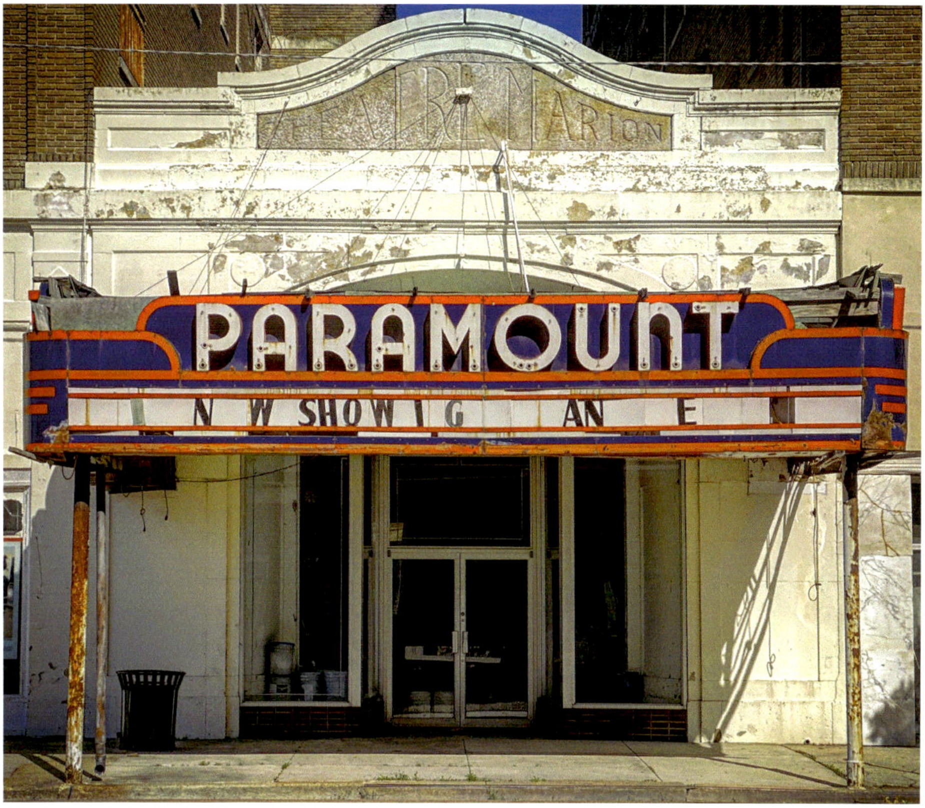

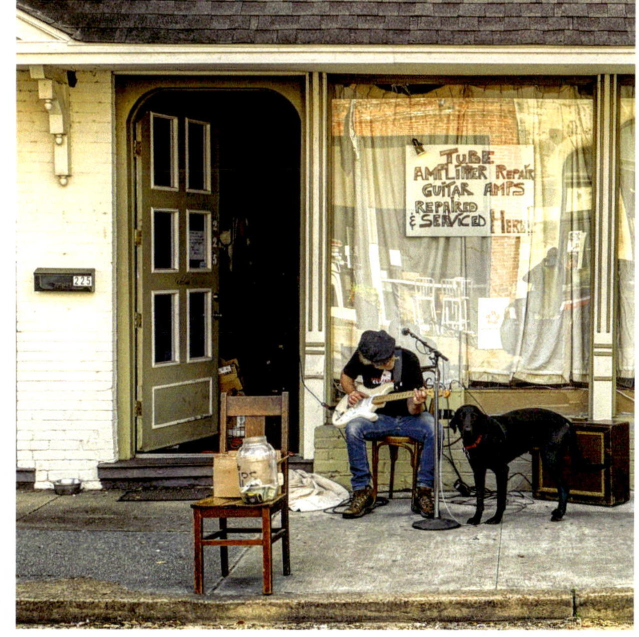

Above: Some say Clarksdale is frozen in time. Unfortunately, the ravages of time are all too apparent on this dilapidated theater.

Right: Many early blues singers used variations on the phrase "going where the Southern cross the Dog." This might be my all-time favorite photo of mine.

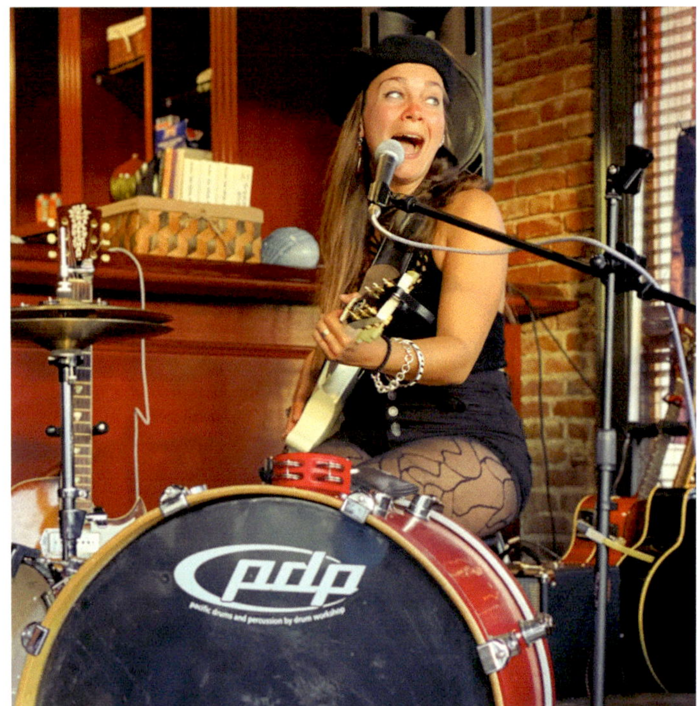

The annual Juke Joint Festival brings musicians and fans from all over the world to Clarkdale. Ghalia Volt is an electrifying one-woman band.

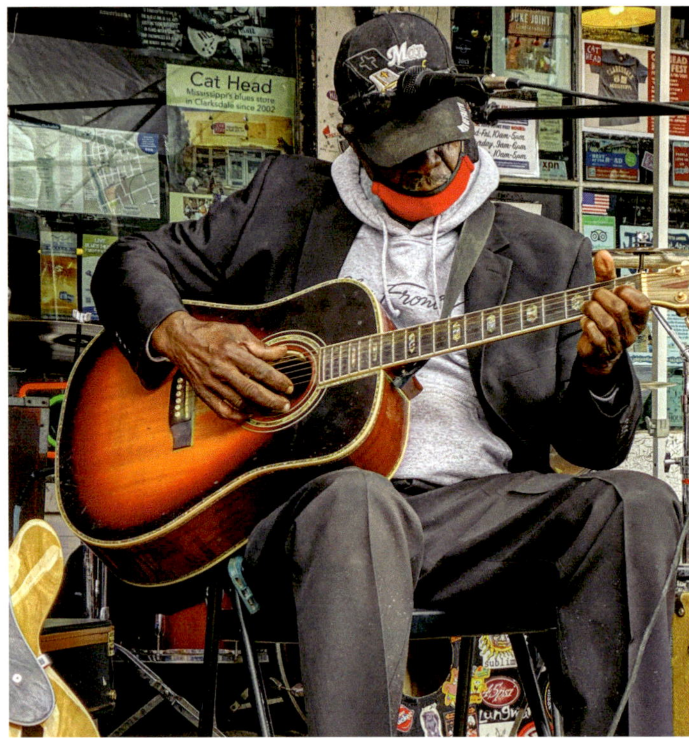

Jimmy "Duck" Holmes is one of the most celebrated musicians alive today and owns the Blue Front Café in Bentonia, MS.

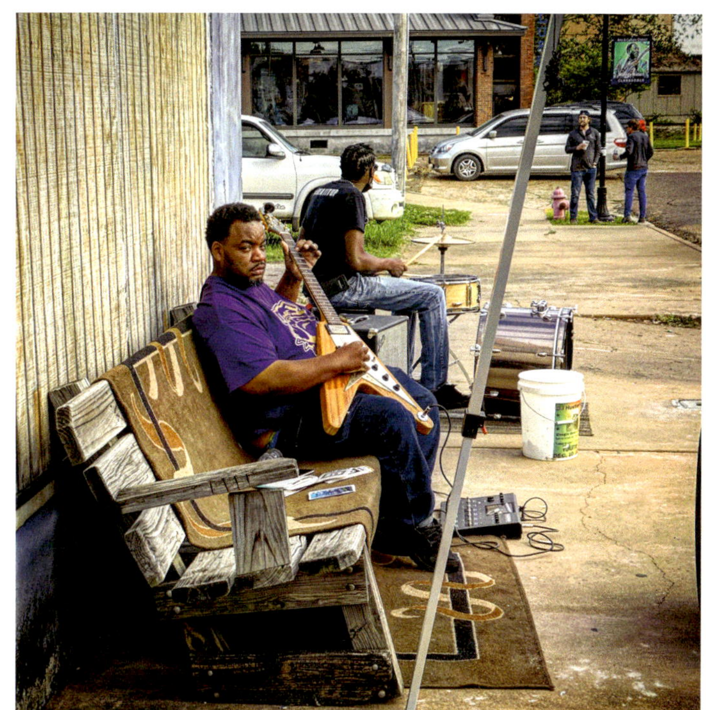

DJ Hustleman plays
one of the swampiest,
funkiest grooves
I've ever heard.

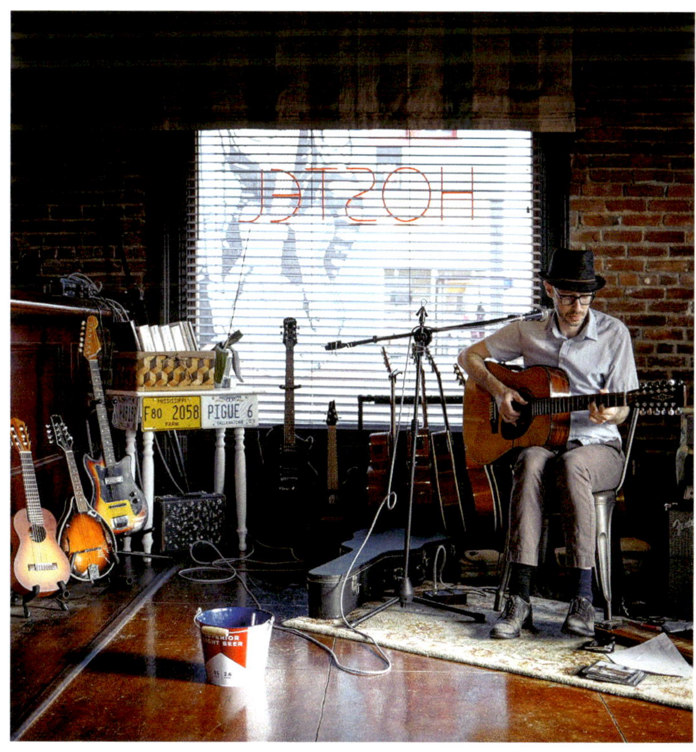

Playing the
Auberge Hostel.

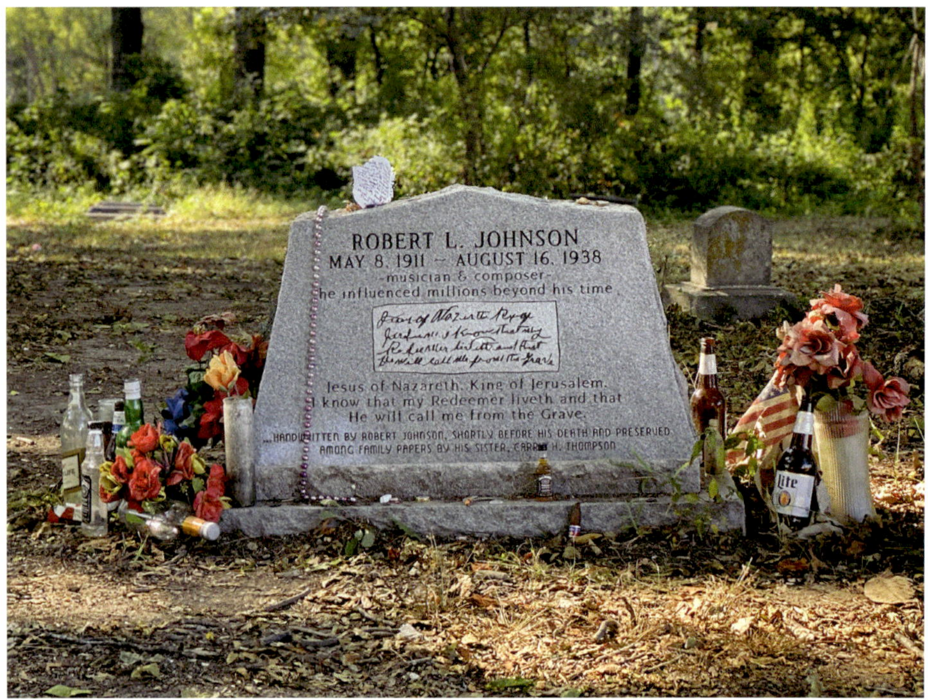

Robert Johnson's grave at Mt. Zion Church, Greenwood, MS.

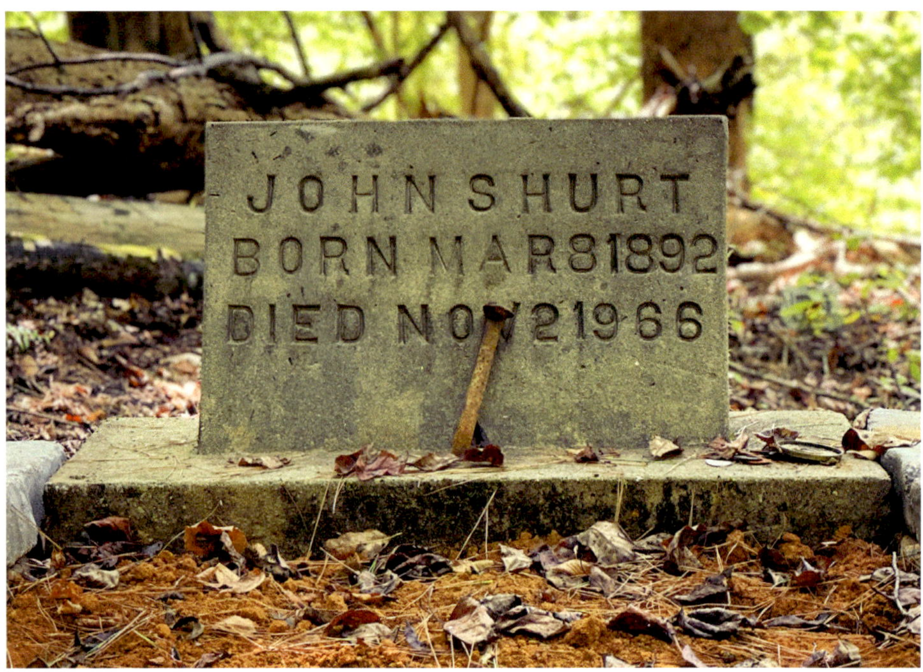

Mississippi John Hurt's grave in Avalon, MS.

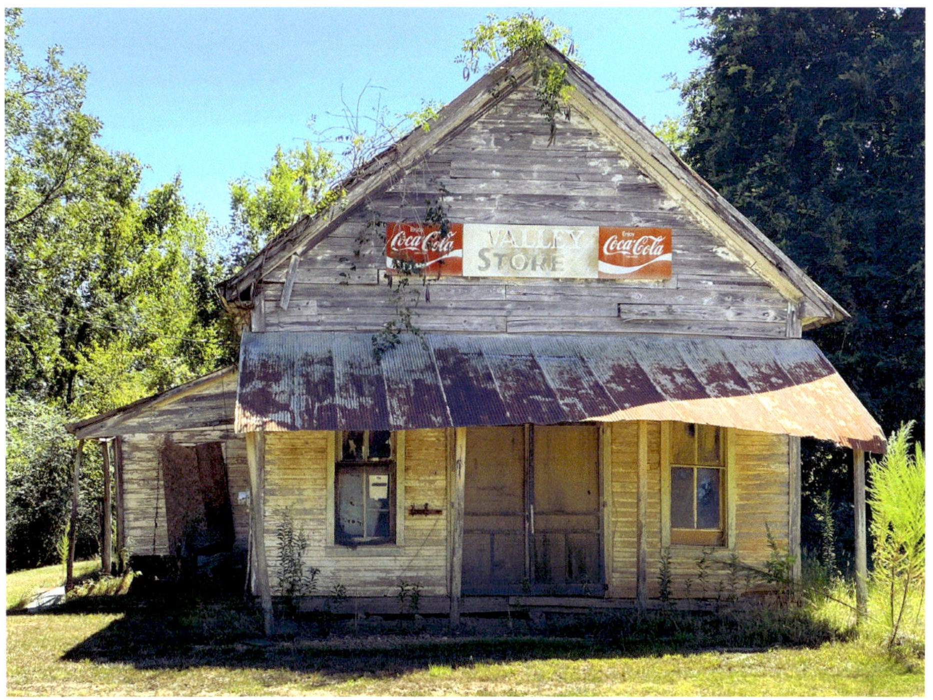

The Valley Store in Avalon, where Mississippi John Hurt entertained.

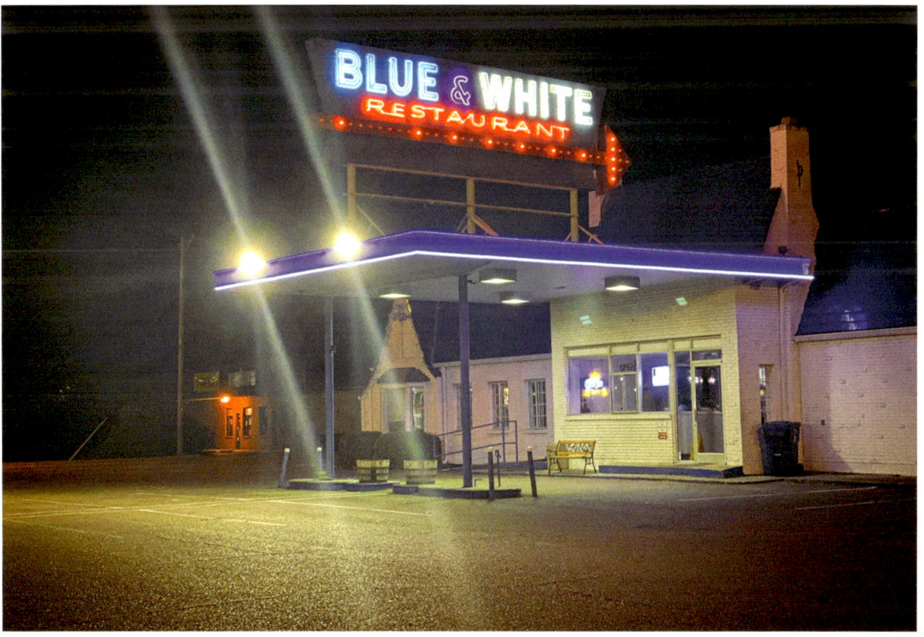

The Blue & White Restaurant in Tunica, MS, on Highway 61. The best damn hamburger steak in the world.

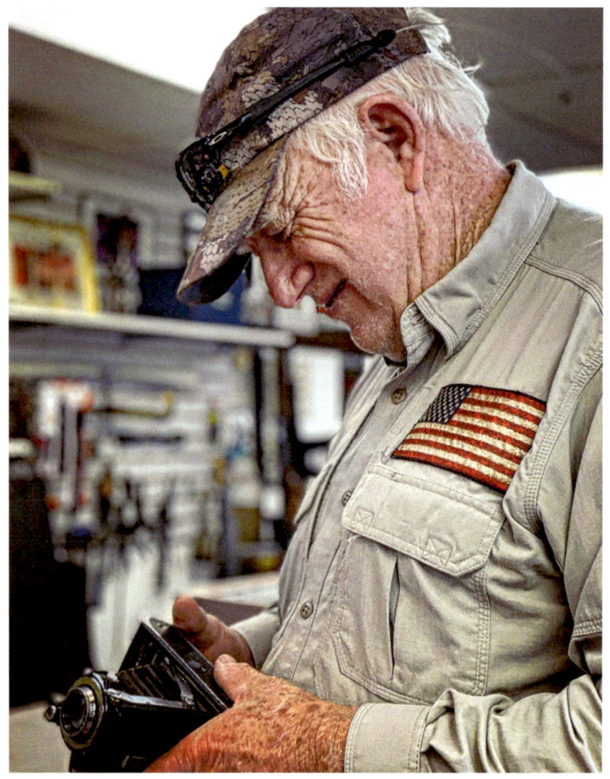

Keller's Pawn Shop, Lake Cormorant, MS, on Highway 61.

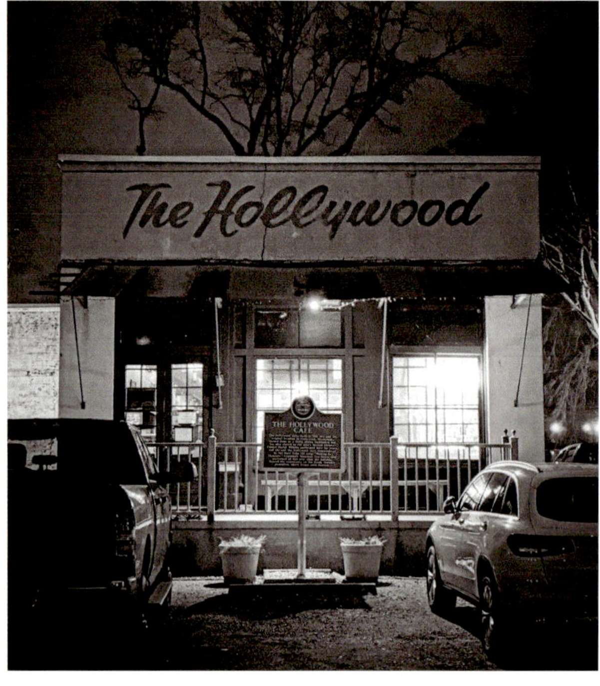

The Hollywood, made famous by Marc Cohn in the song "Walking in Memphis." Southern dining the way it was meant to be.

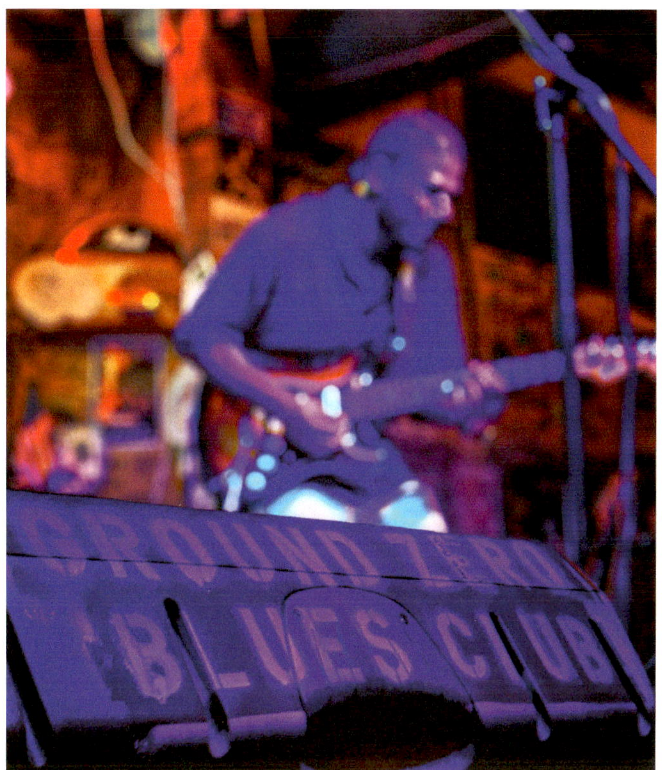

Big Anthony Sherrod at
Ground Zero Blues Club.

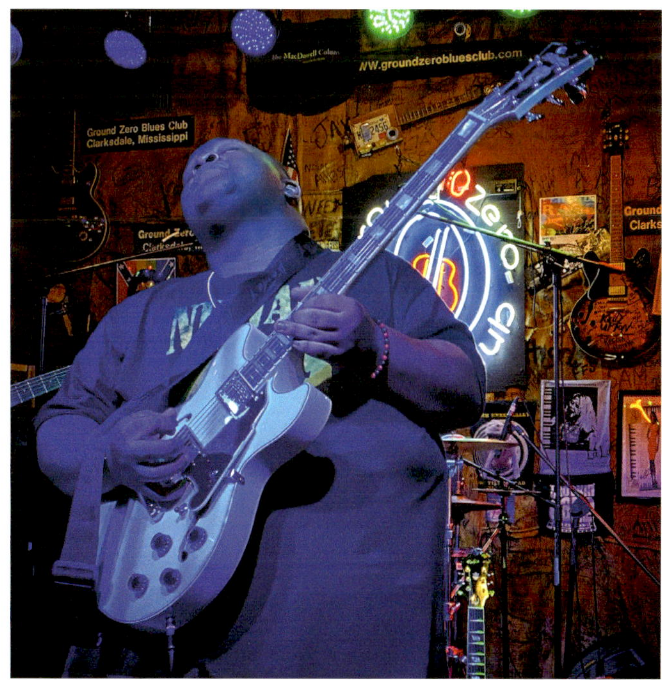

Chirstone "Kingfish"
Ingram, who many
consider to be the future
of Blues guitar, performing
at Ground Zero Blues Club.

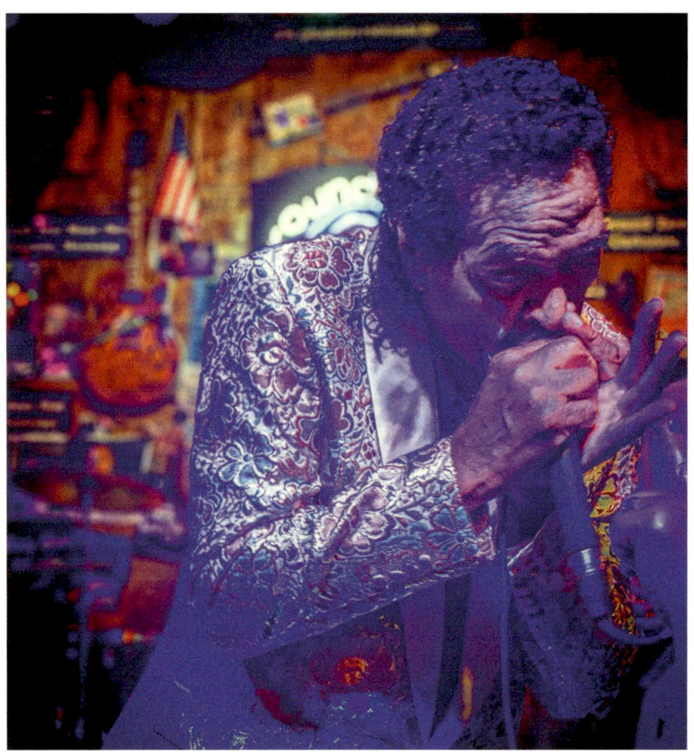

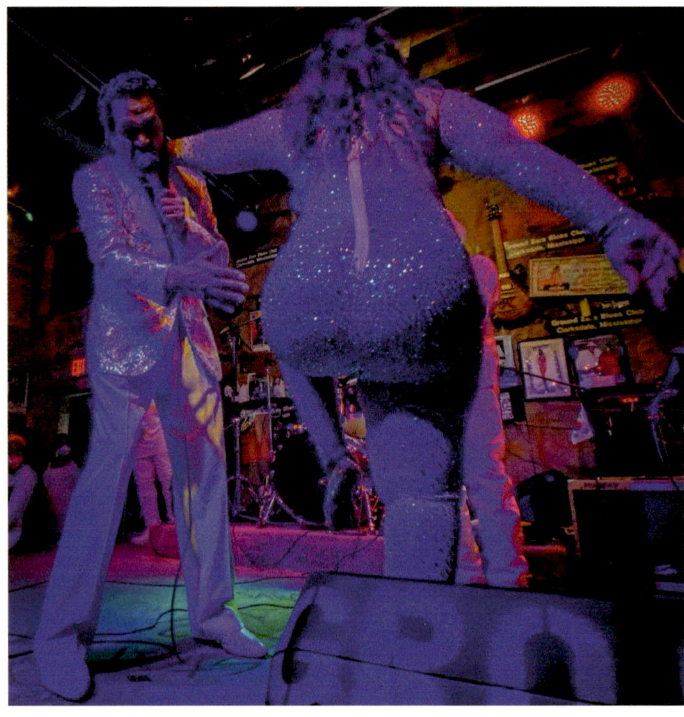

Music legend Bobby
Rush performing at
Ground Zero Blues Club.
One of the very best
concerts I've ever seen.

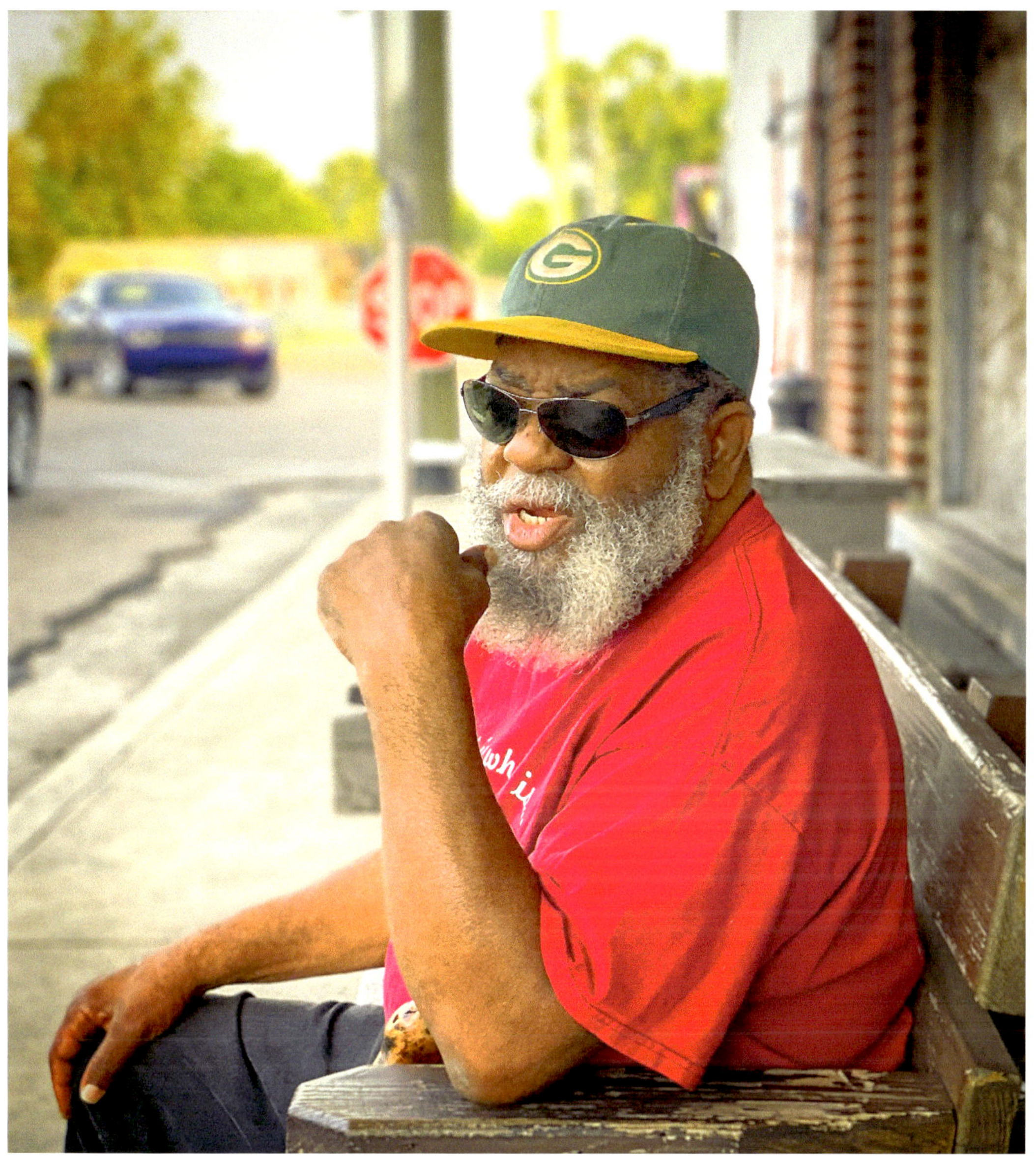

The late great Red Paden. Owner of Red's Lounge. Gone, but never forgotten.

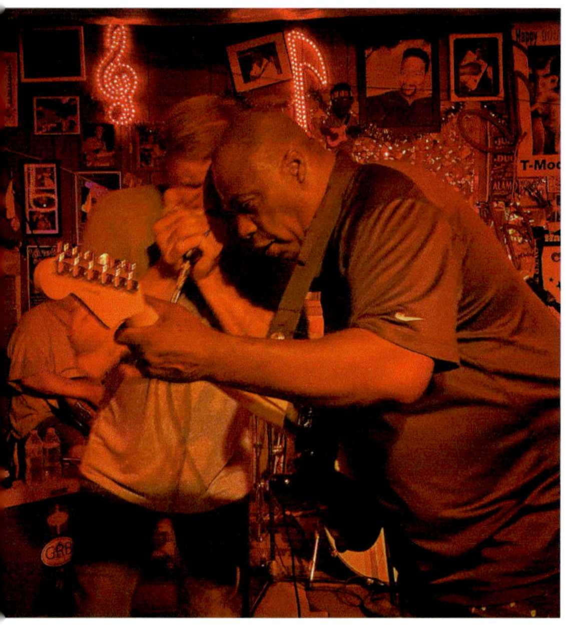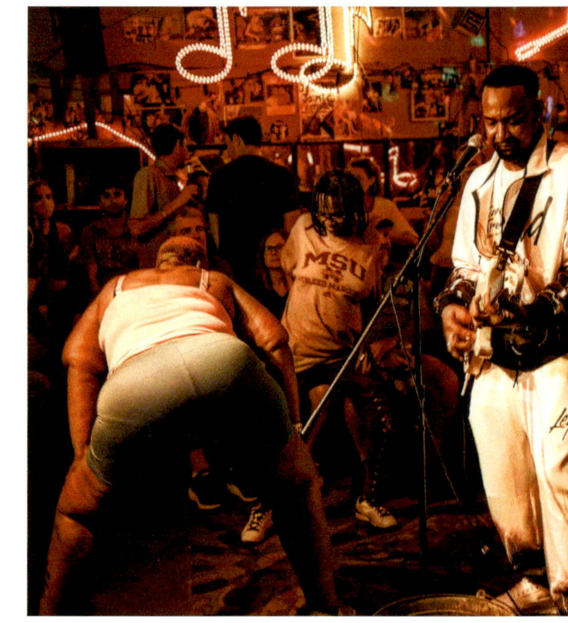

Red's Lounge.

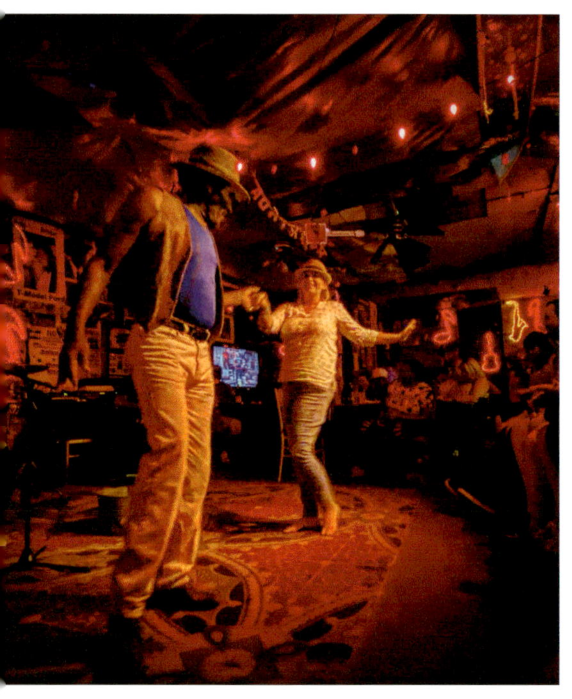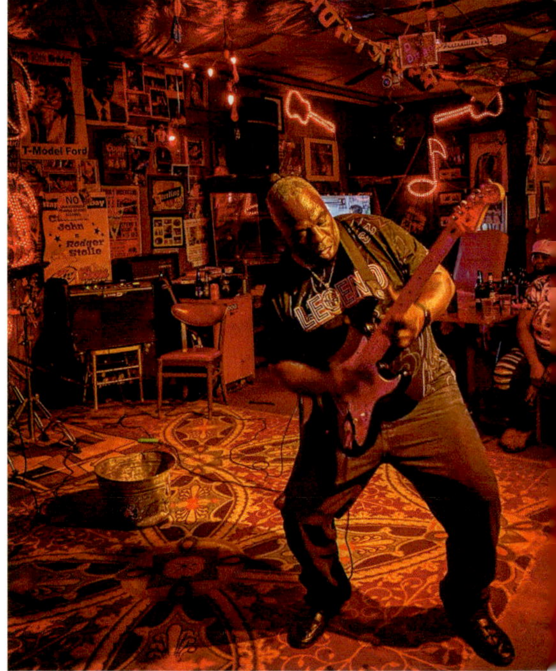

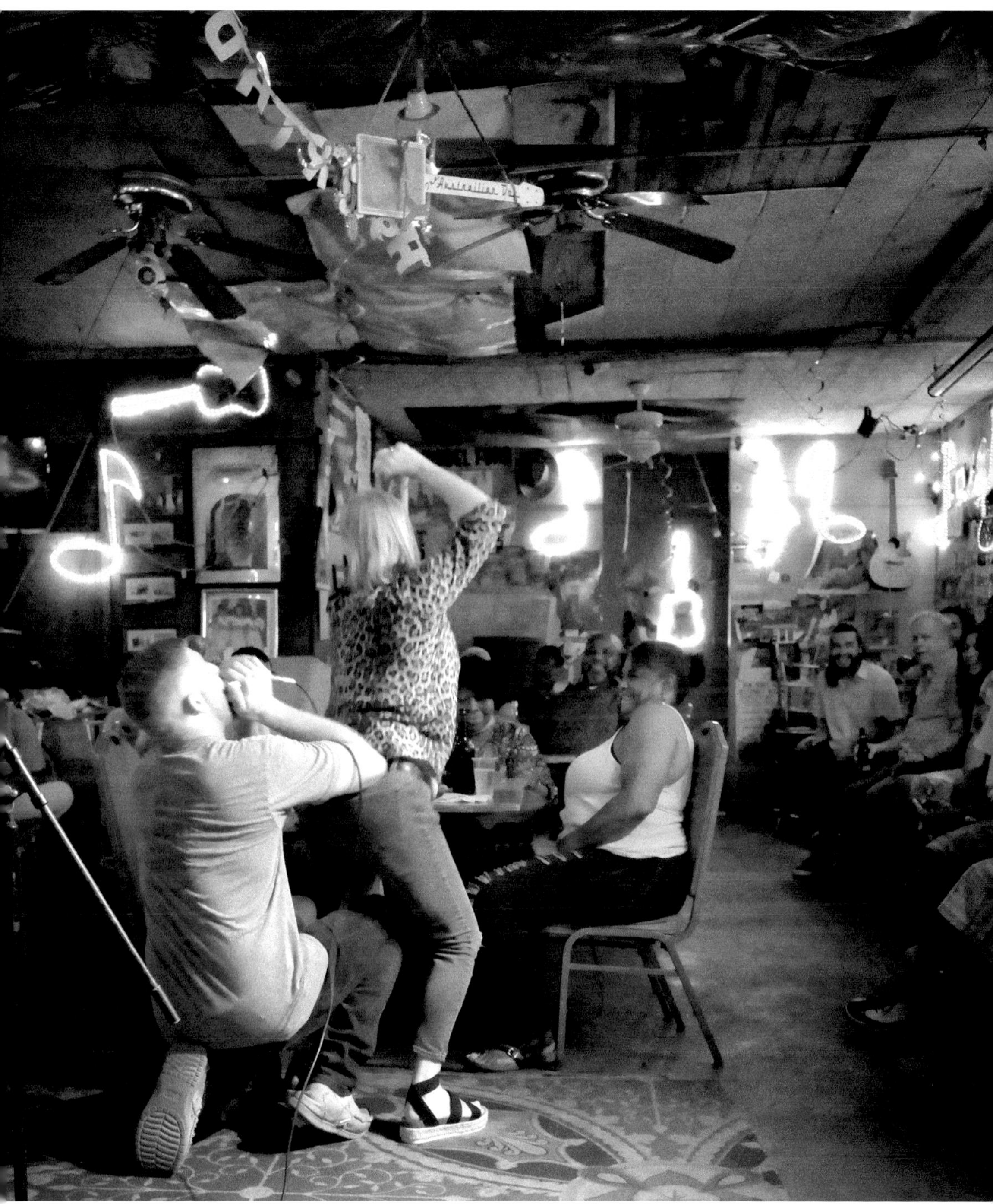

Blowing harp. (Fun fact: that's the harp player's wife.)

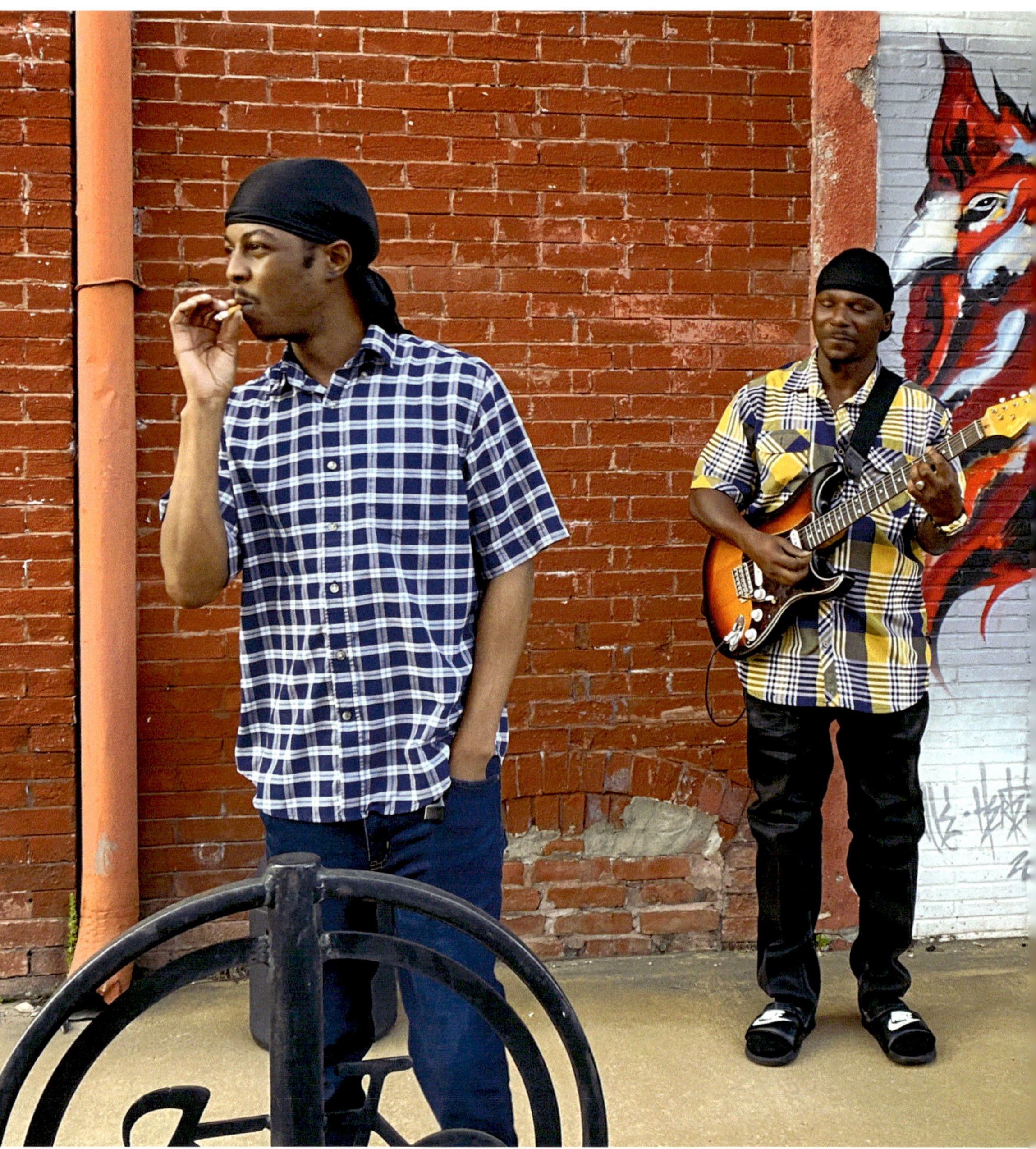

Lee and Big A busking on the street, promoting their show.

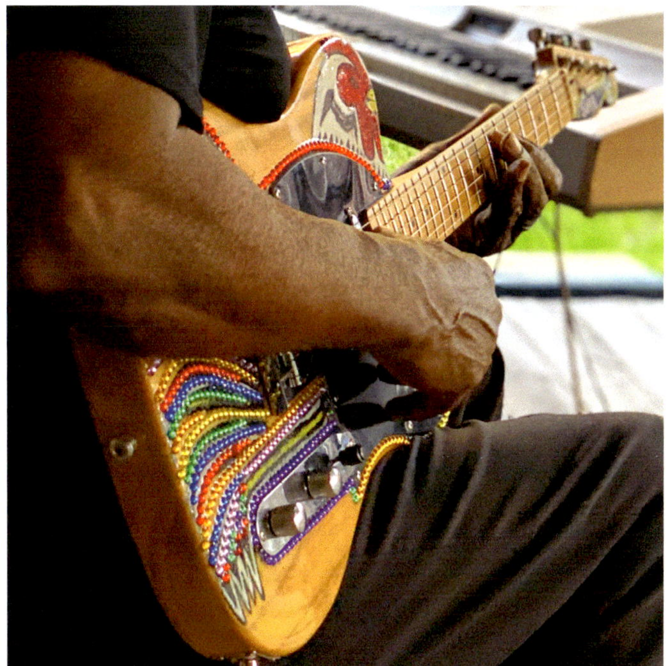

Right: James "Super Chikan" Johnson.

Below: The author's sister, eating cotton. As one does.

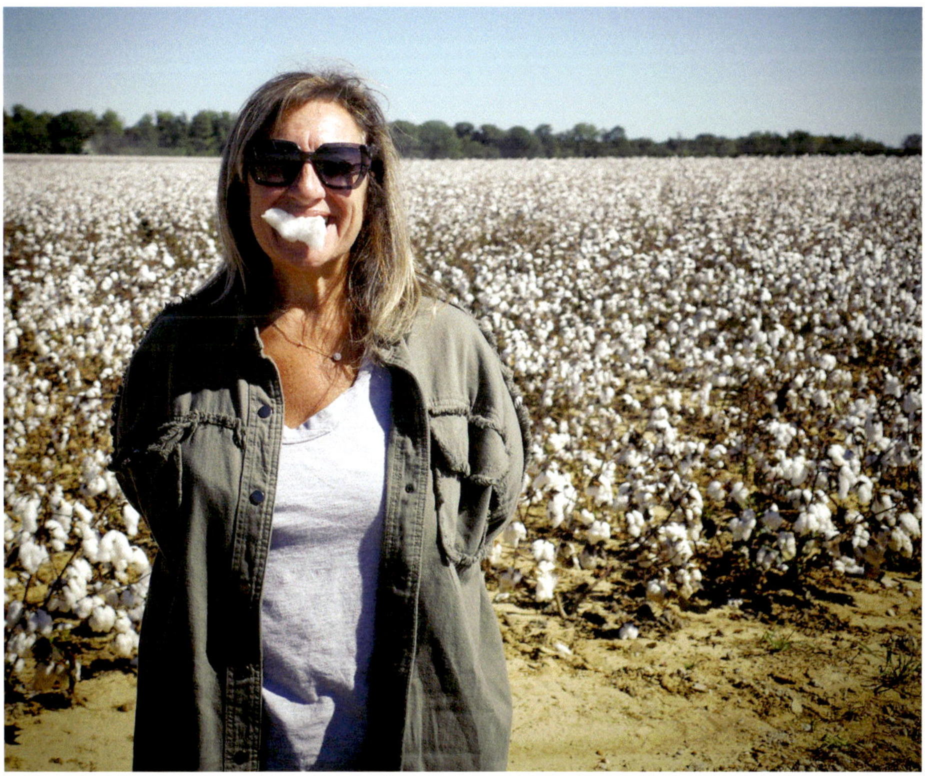

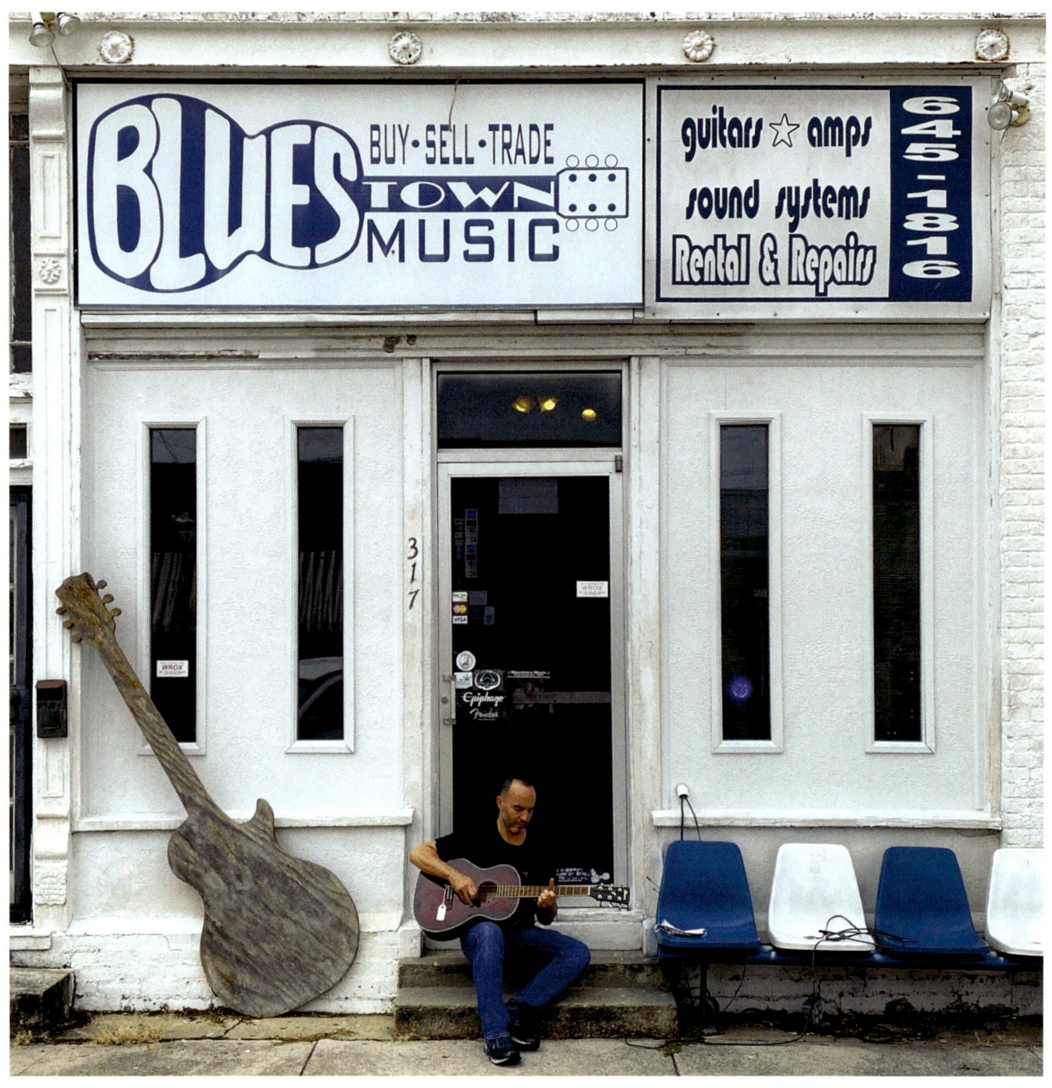

Your humble author, playing on the steps of a Clarksdale music store.

5

Tom Lee Park

Memphis has many problems. Gang-related crime and gun violence are up. There isn't sufficient funding for infrastructure and education. It has one of the highest poverty rates in the country, and there's far too much substandard housing.

But Memphis constantly has proven that no matter how many times it takes a hit, it gets back up and continues to rise to face all challenges.

The renovated Tom Lee Park finally opened in September 2023. It features fields, a sunset deck, basketball courts with a sunset canopy honoring Tyre Nichols's memory, miniature golf, a gorgeous children's playground, and more.

When it opened, many Memphians commented that they expected the city's investment in this public space would quickly go to waste. Predictions that a fatality, robberies, and theft would occur within weeks and make the park undesirable for locals were all too common—and reasonable to make.

As it turns out, the people of Memphis are dedicated to making Tom Lee Park work. The city's investment in the community seems to be paying off. As of this writing, it remains popular, safe, and welcoming to everyone. I go down most nights to witness the sunset over the Old Bridge, watch people play pickup basketball, and take their children to the playground. It's Memphis at its very best.

I've chosen to close this book with scenes of people enjoying this public space. It's the perfect way to show the gritty resilience and optimism of Memphians. The city's best days are still ahead. I'm so excited to be here to witness the evolution, be part of this community, and call the Home of the Blues my home.

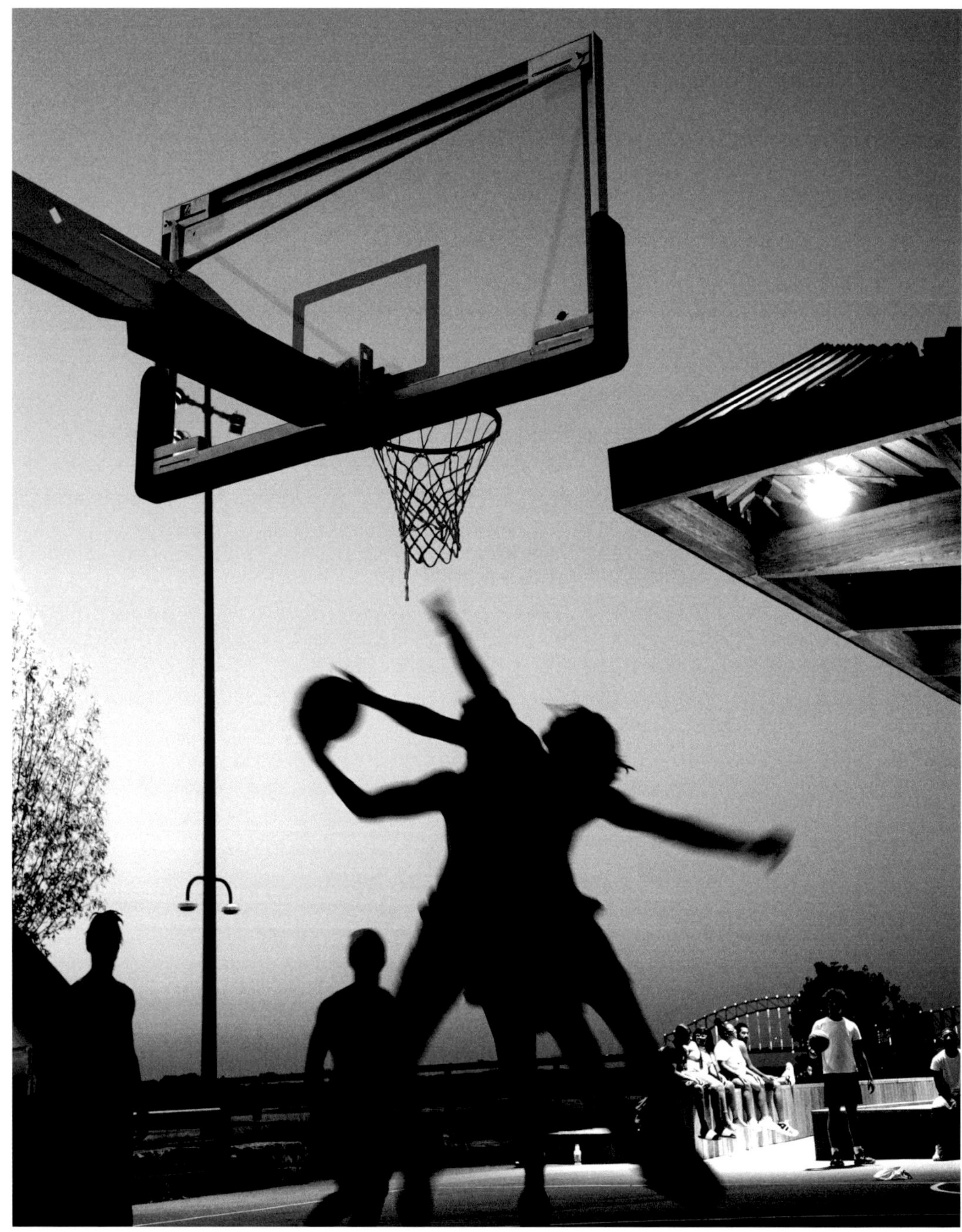

Above and opposite page: From nightly pickup basketball games to occasional dance classes, Tom Lee Park is Memphis at its best.

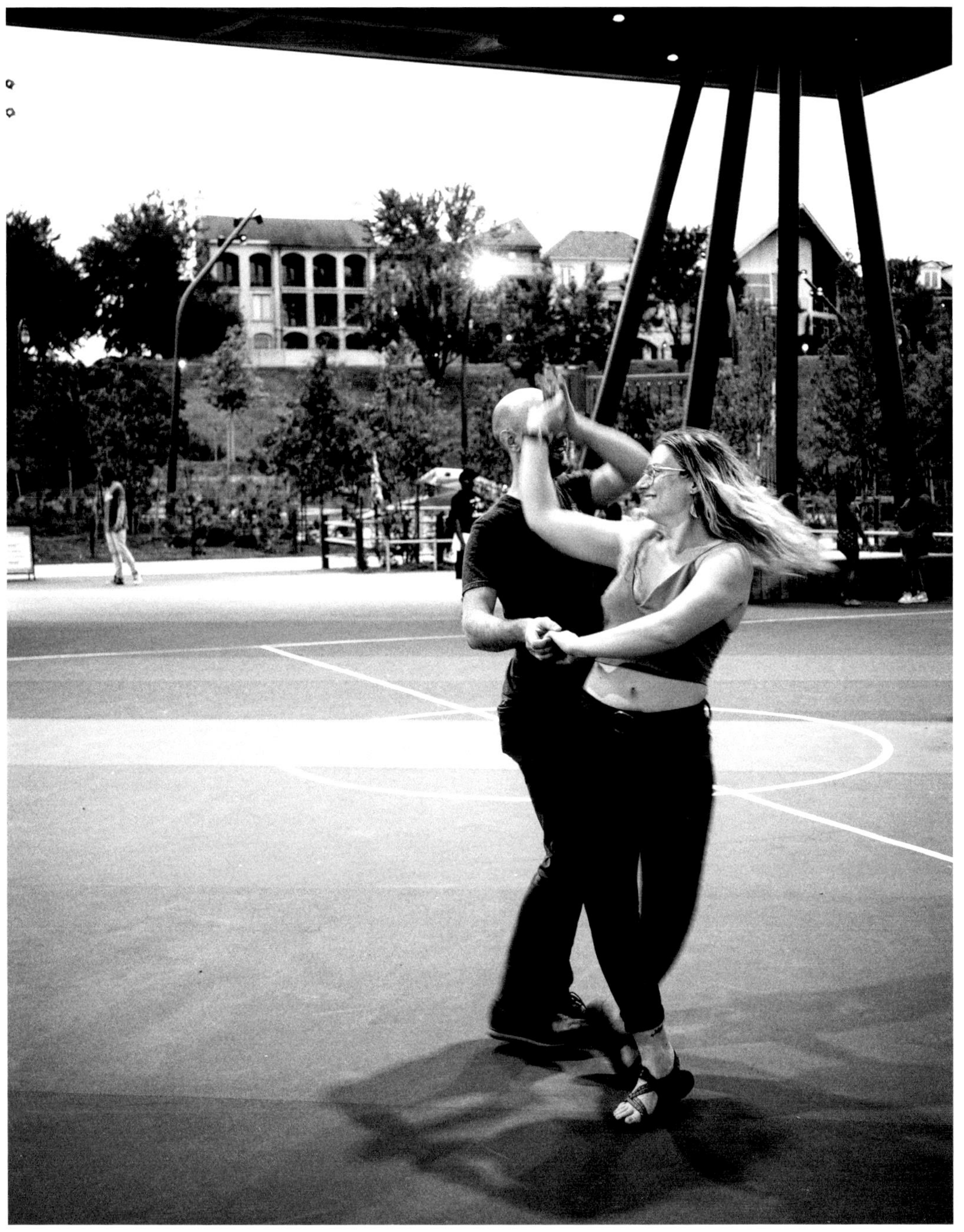

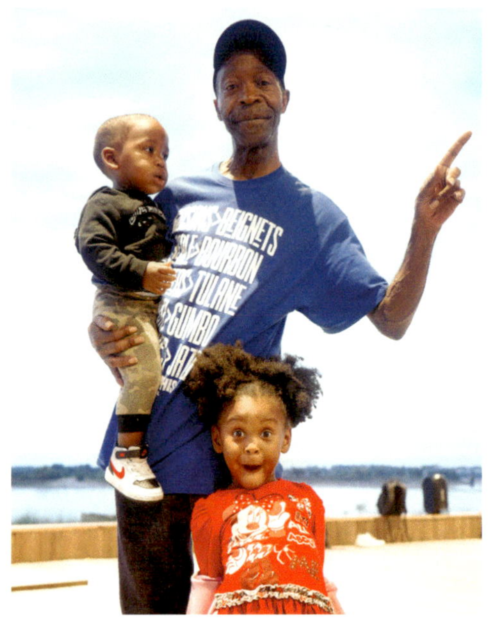

Family time at and in the vicinity of Tom Lee Park.

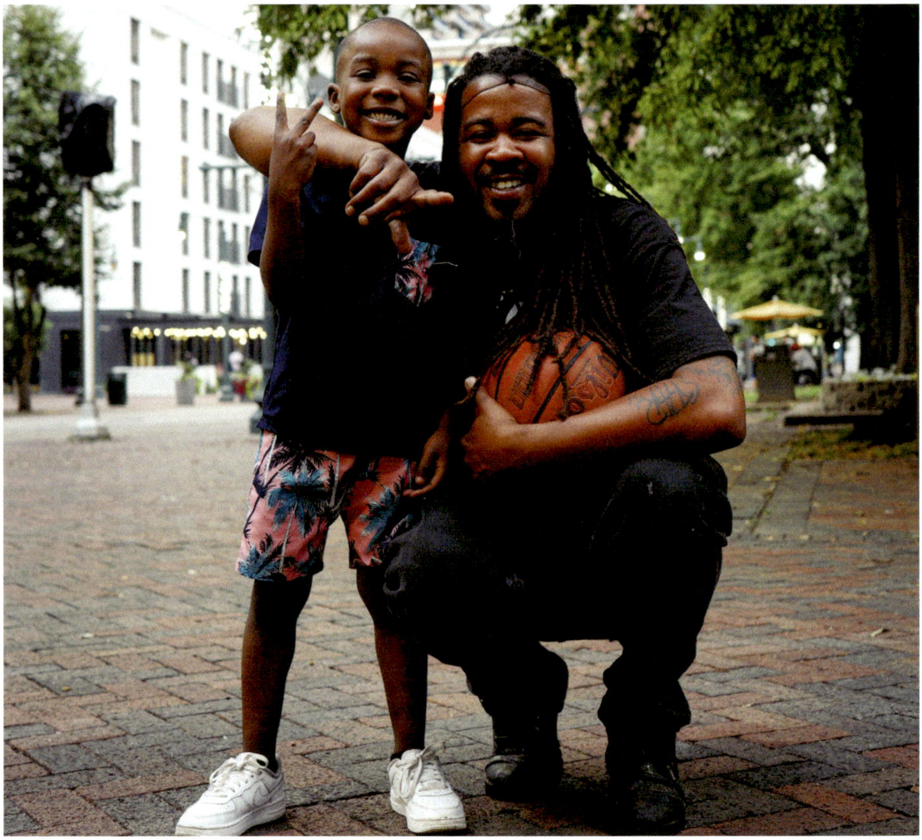

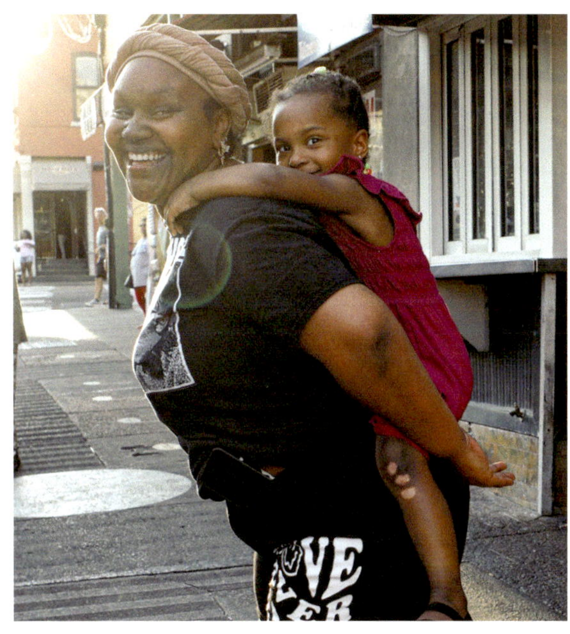

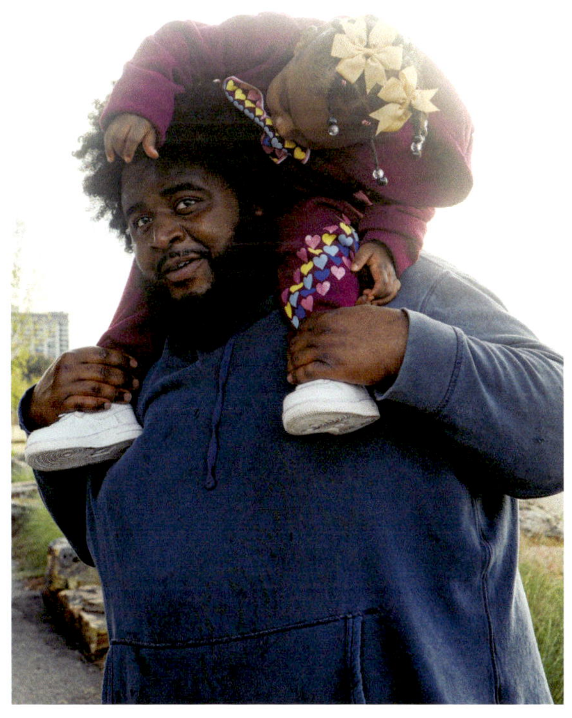

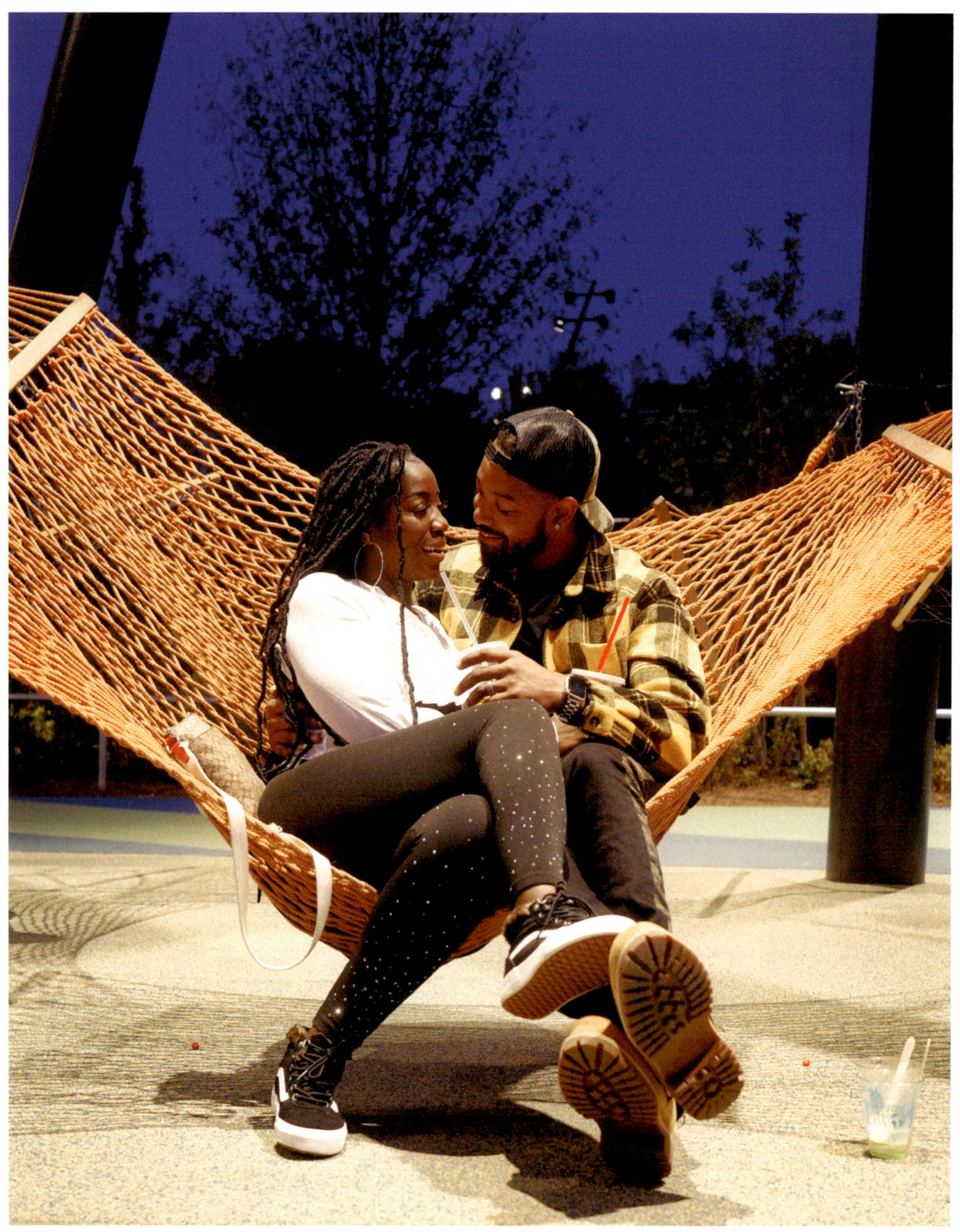

Quality time together at the park.

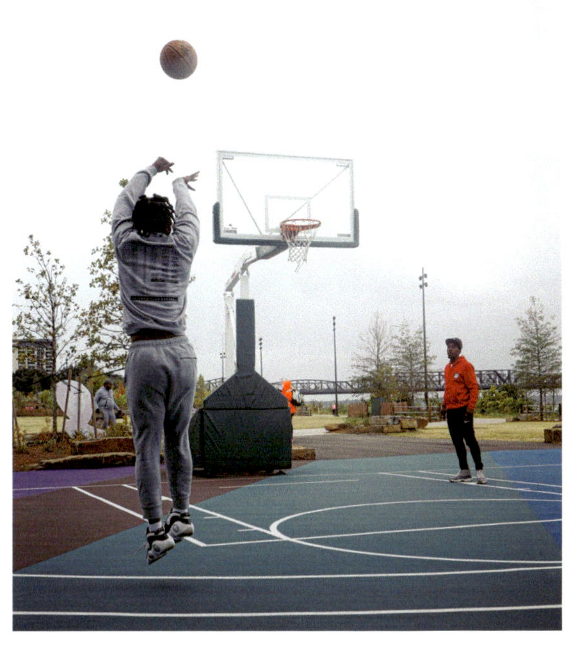

Shooting hoops.

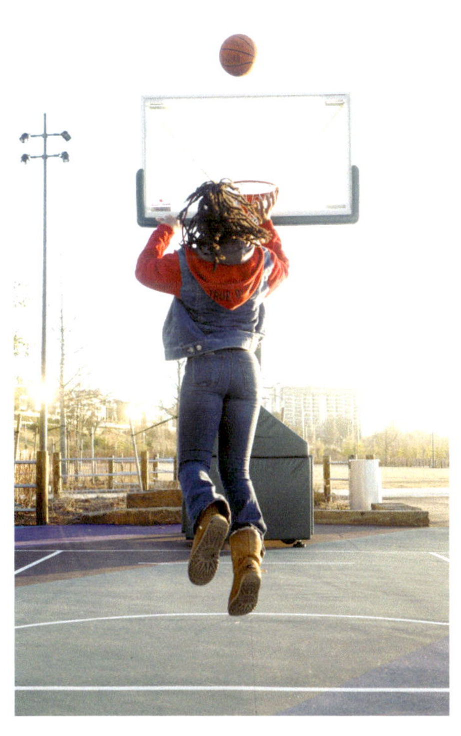

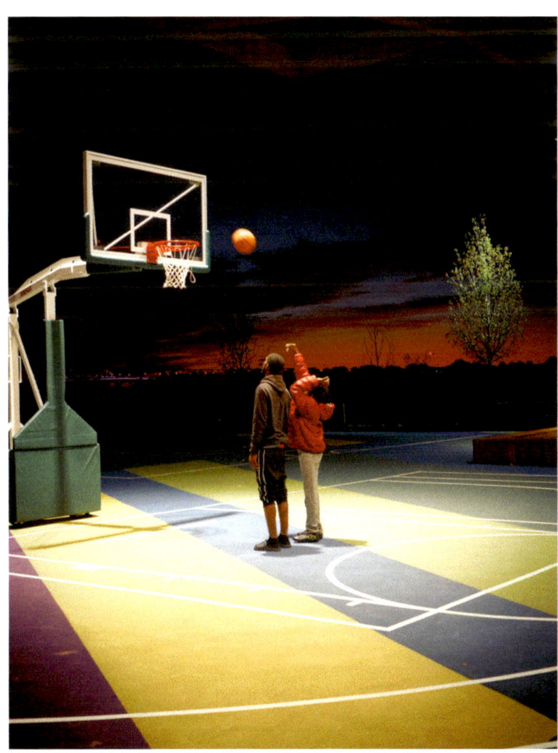

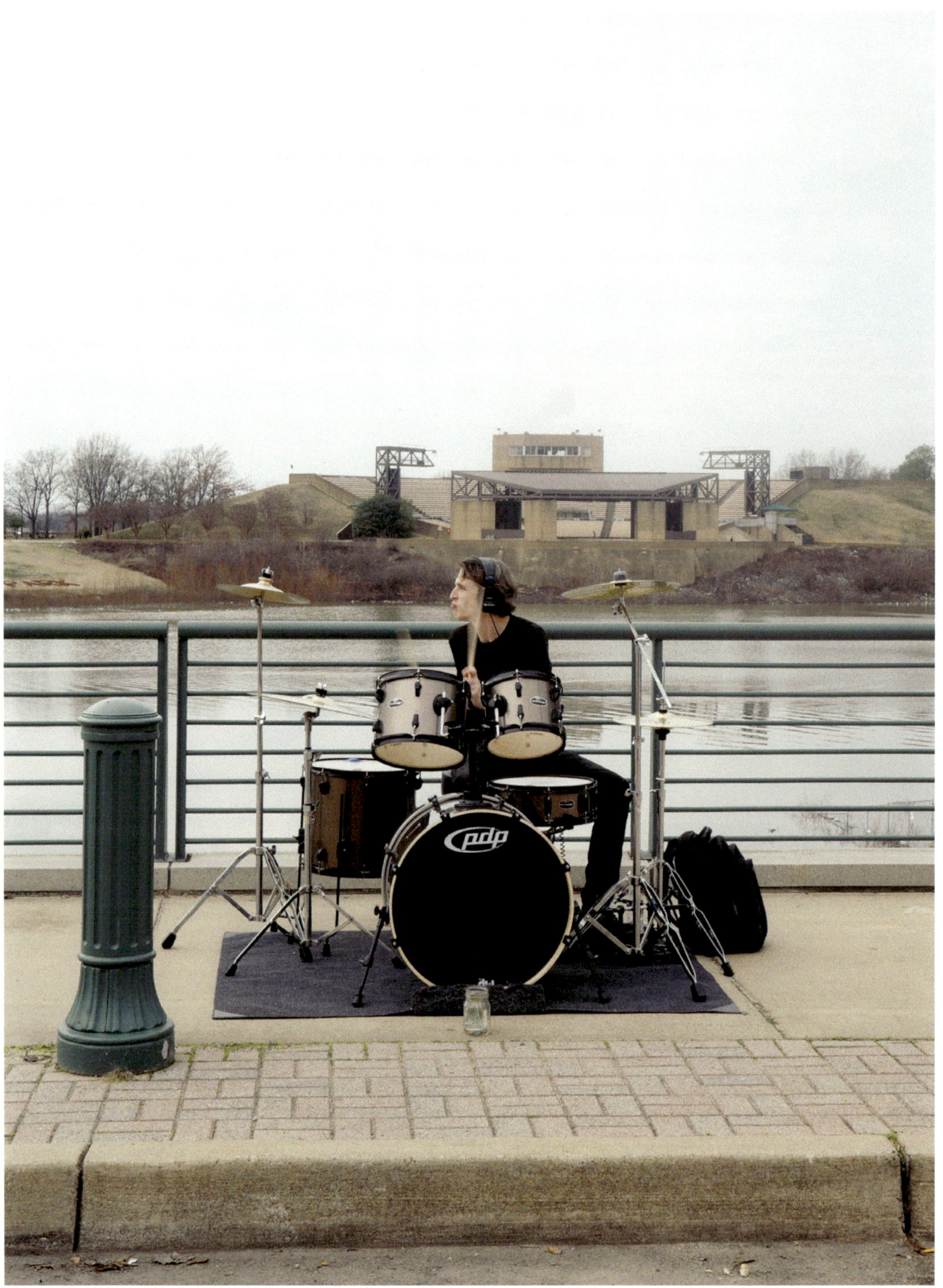

Of course, someone schlepped his entire drum kit to Riverside Drive in front of the park. It's Memphis!

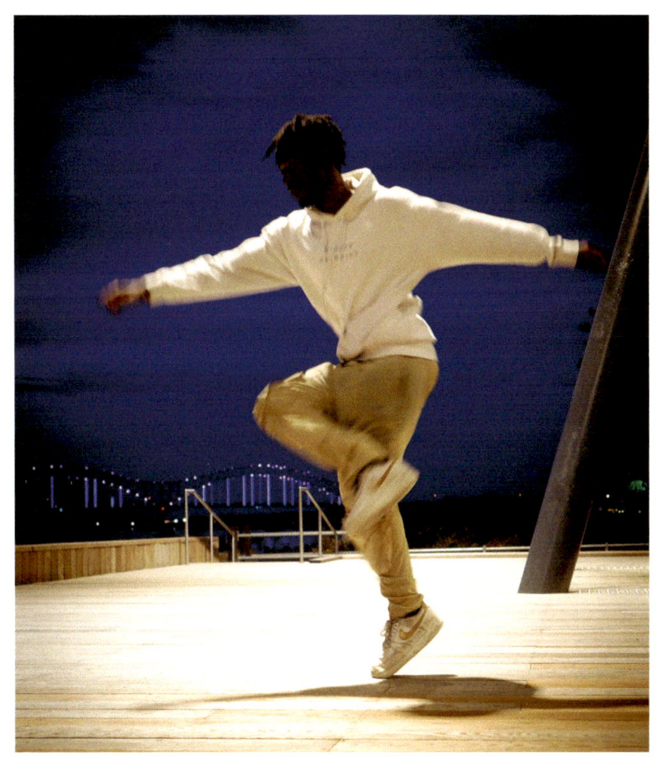

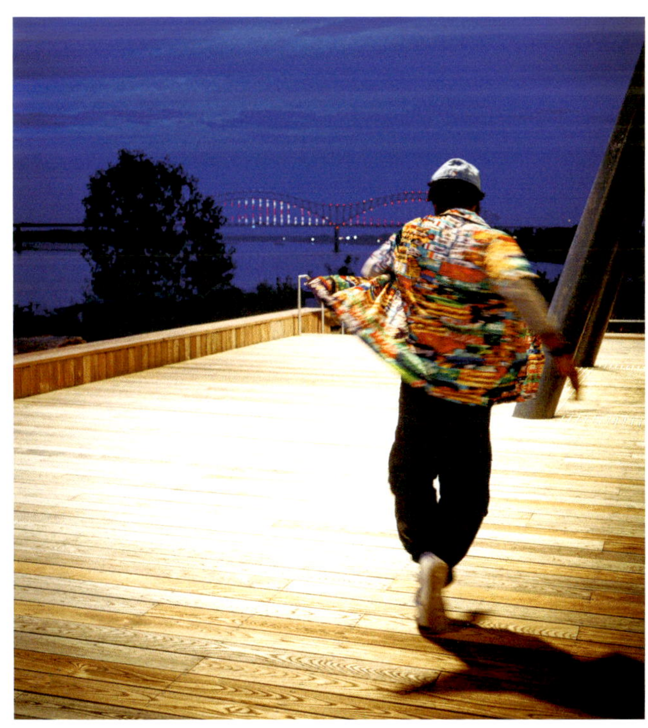

Jookin'.

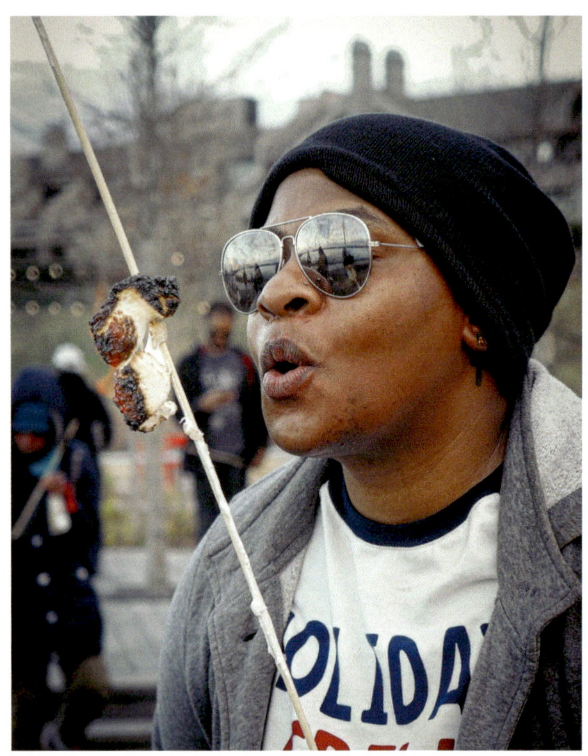

Preparing S'mores to beat the chilly December weather.

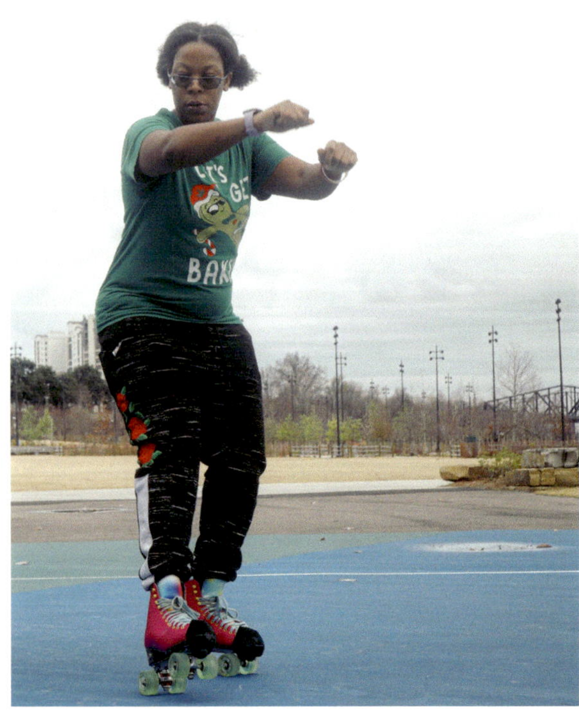

Skateboarding has gained renewed popularity in the 901.

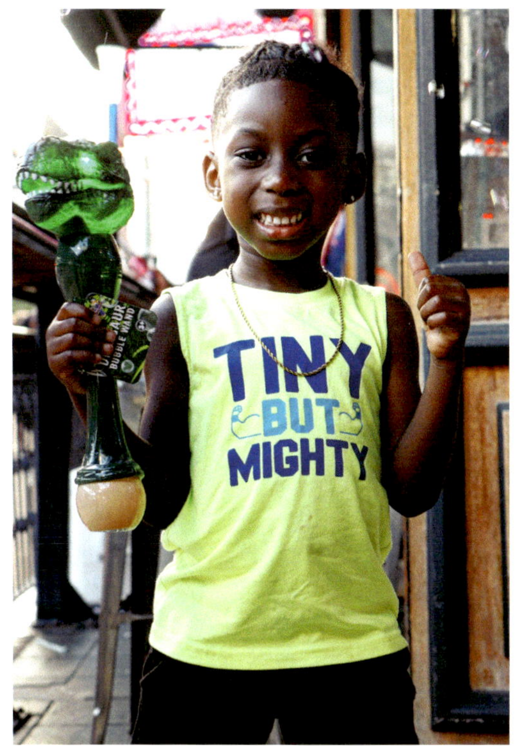
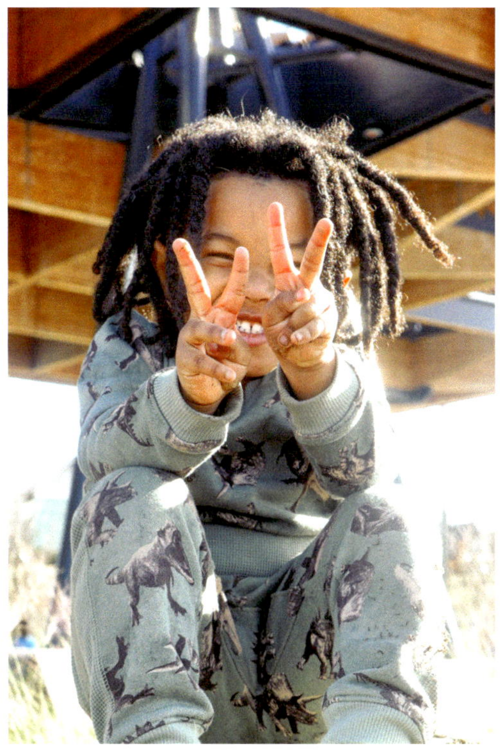

The kids are alright, and Memphis's future is in good hands.

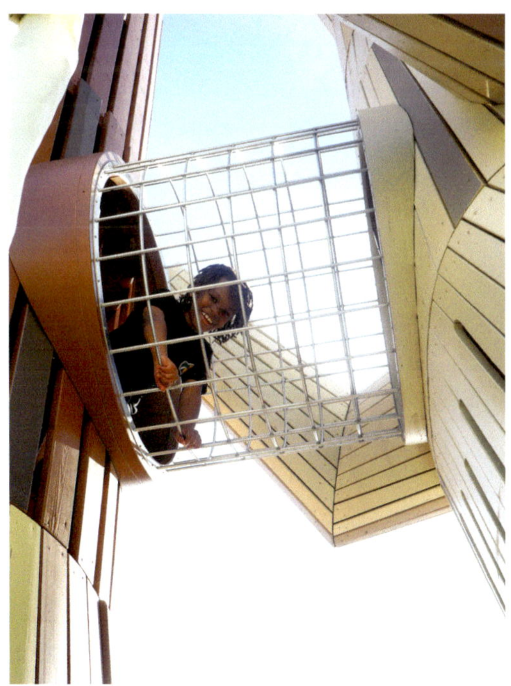
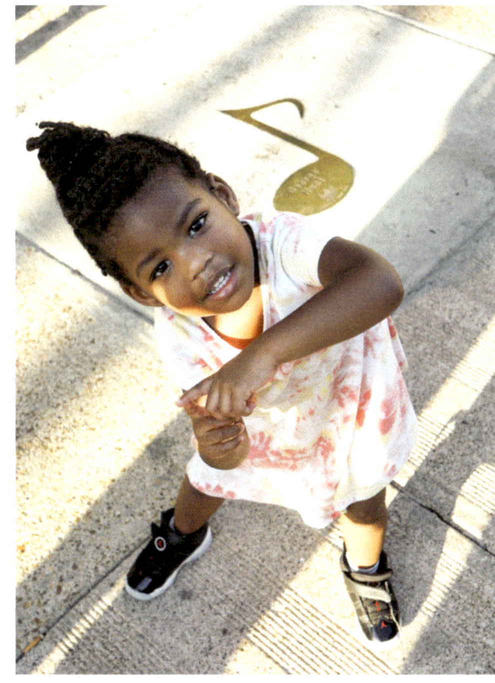

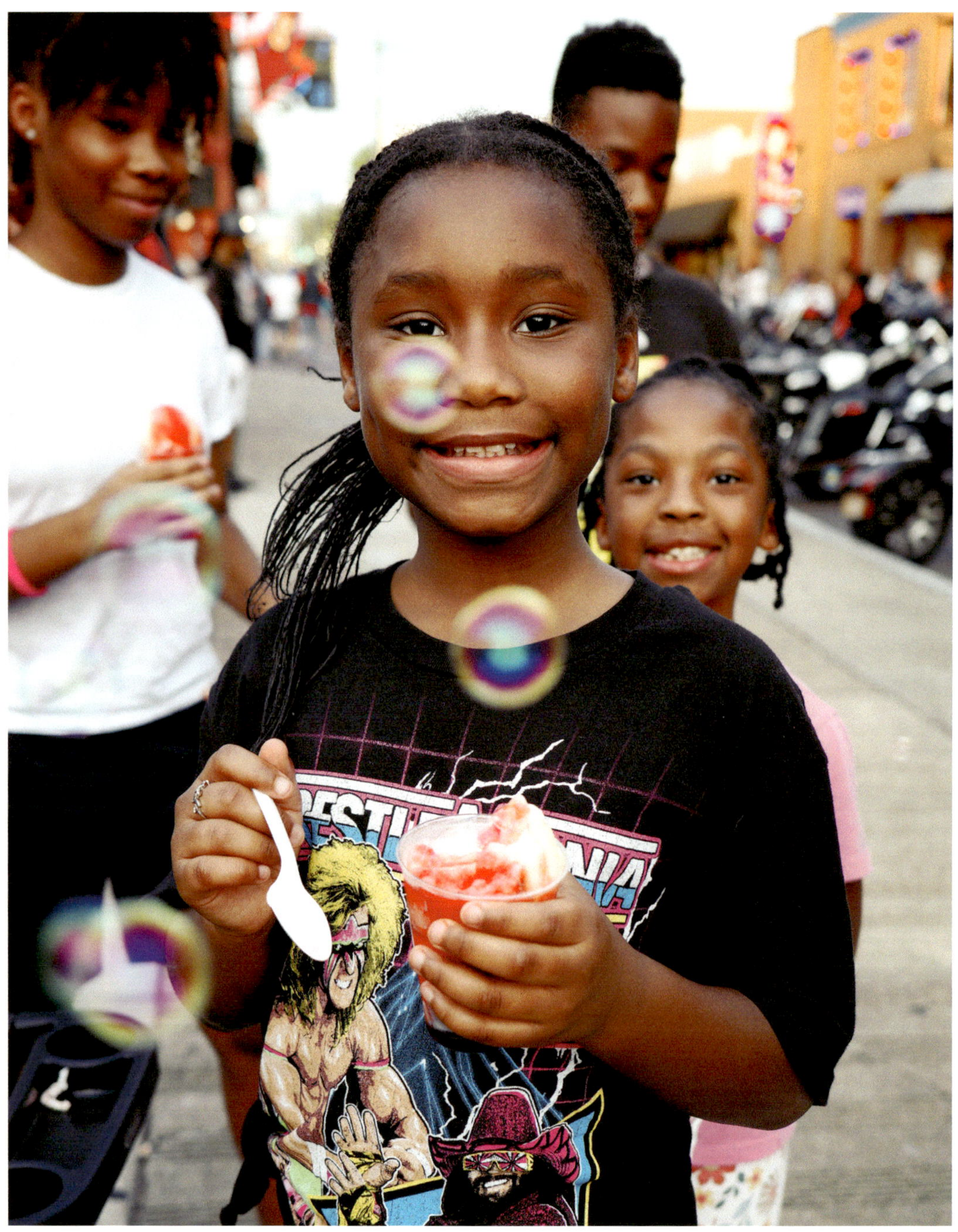

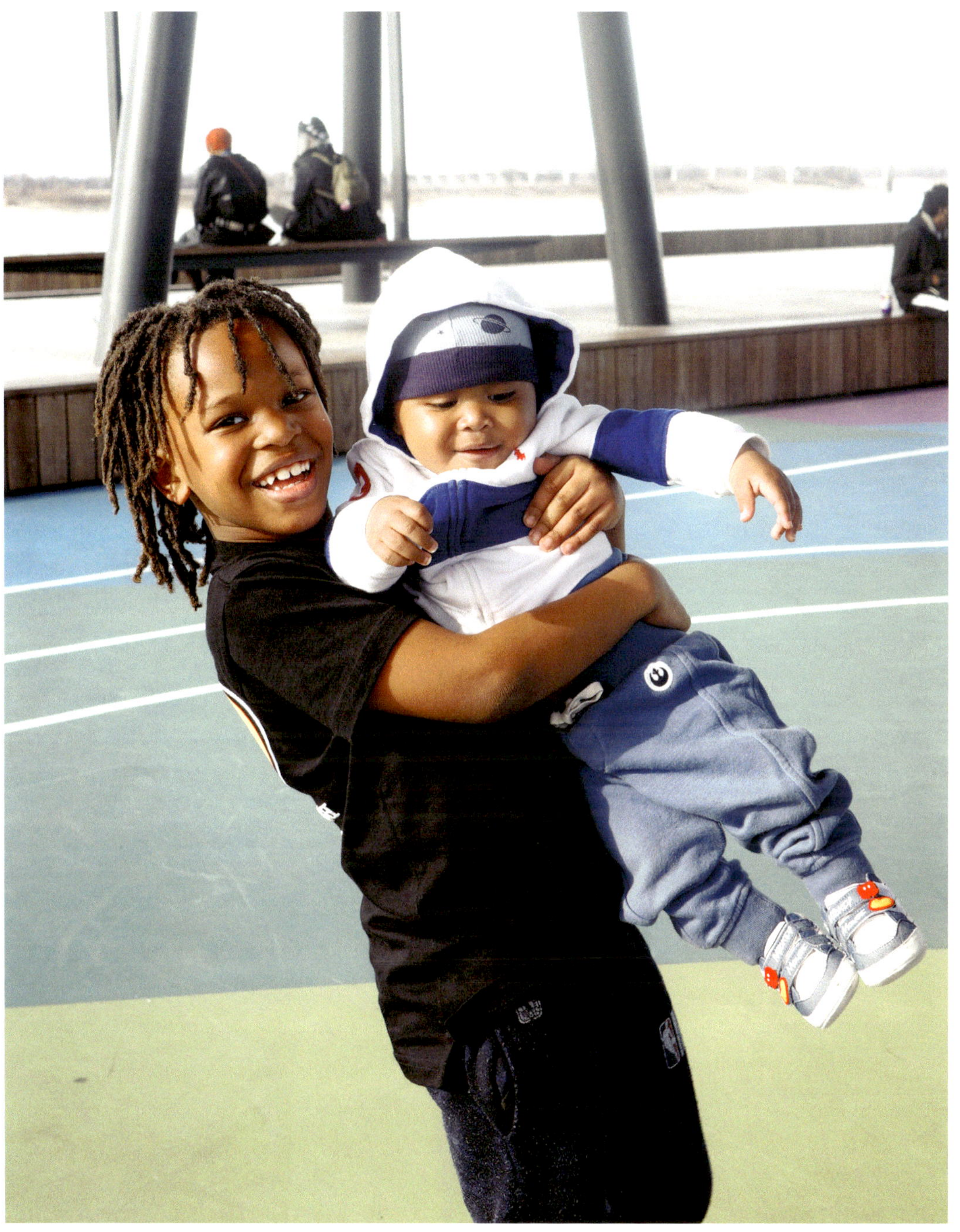

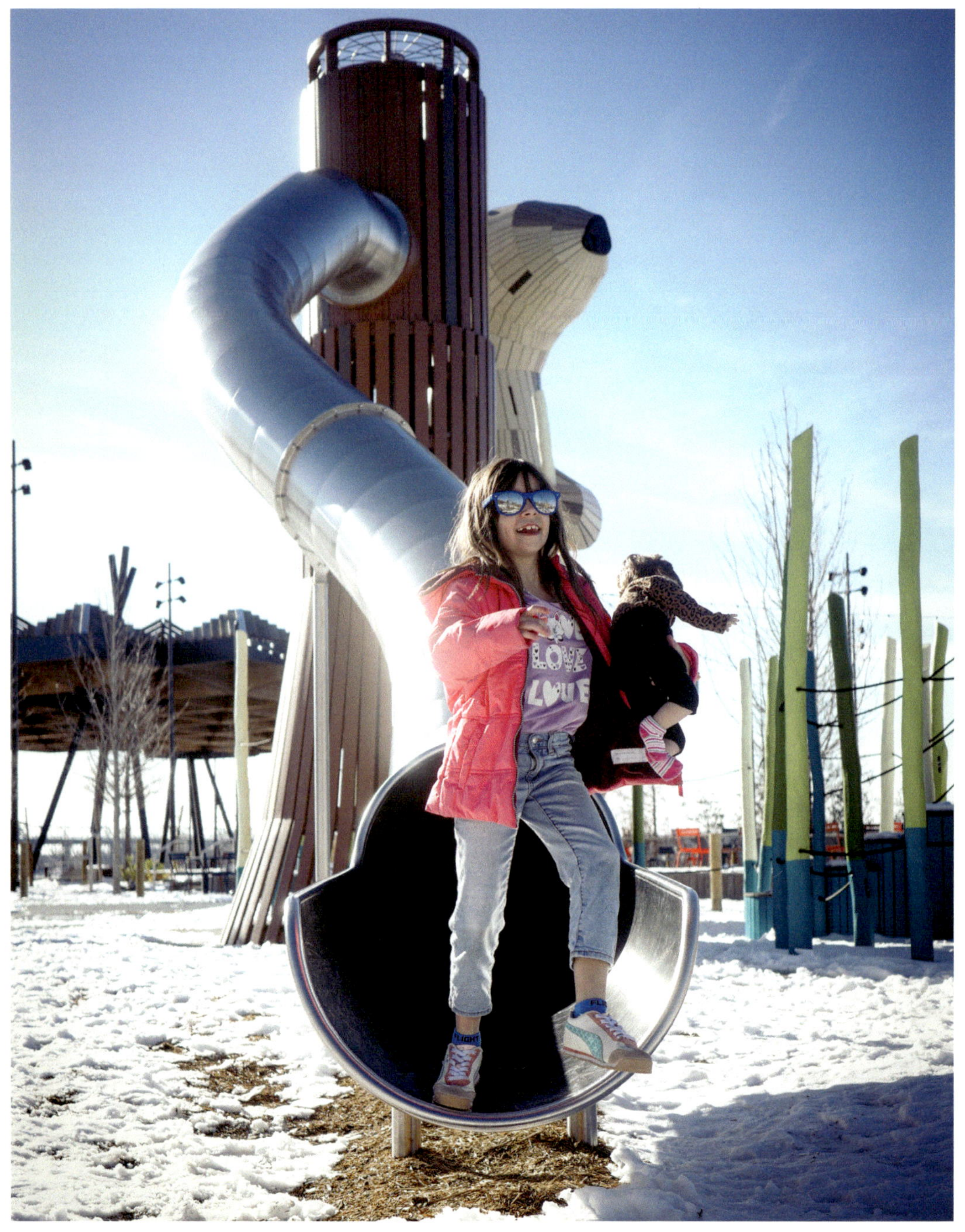

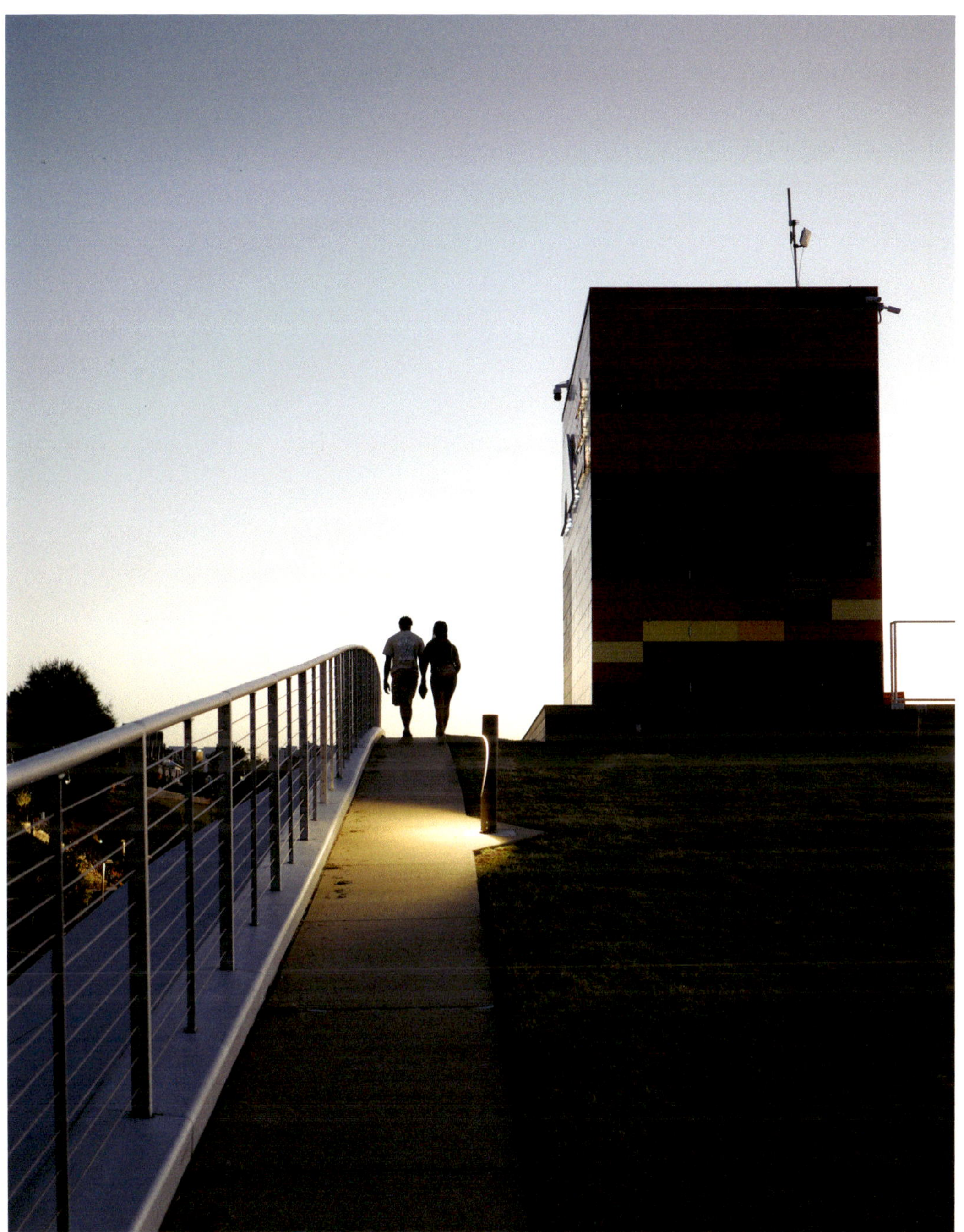

Meditative night stroll.

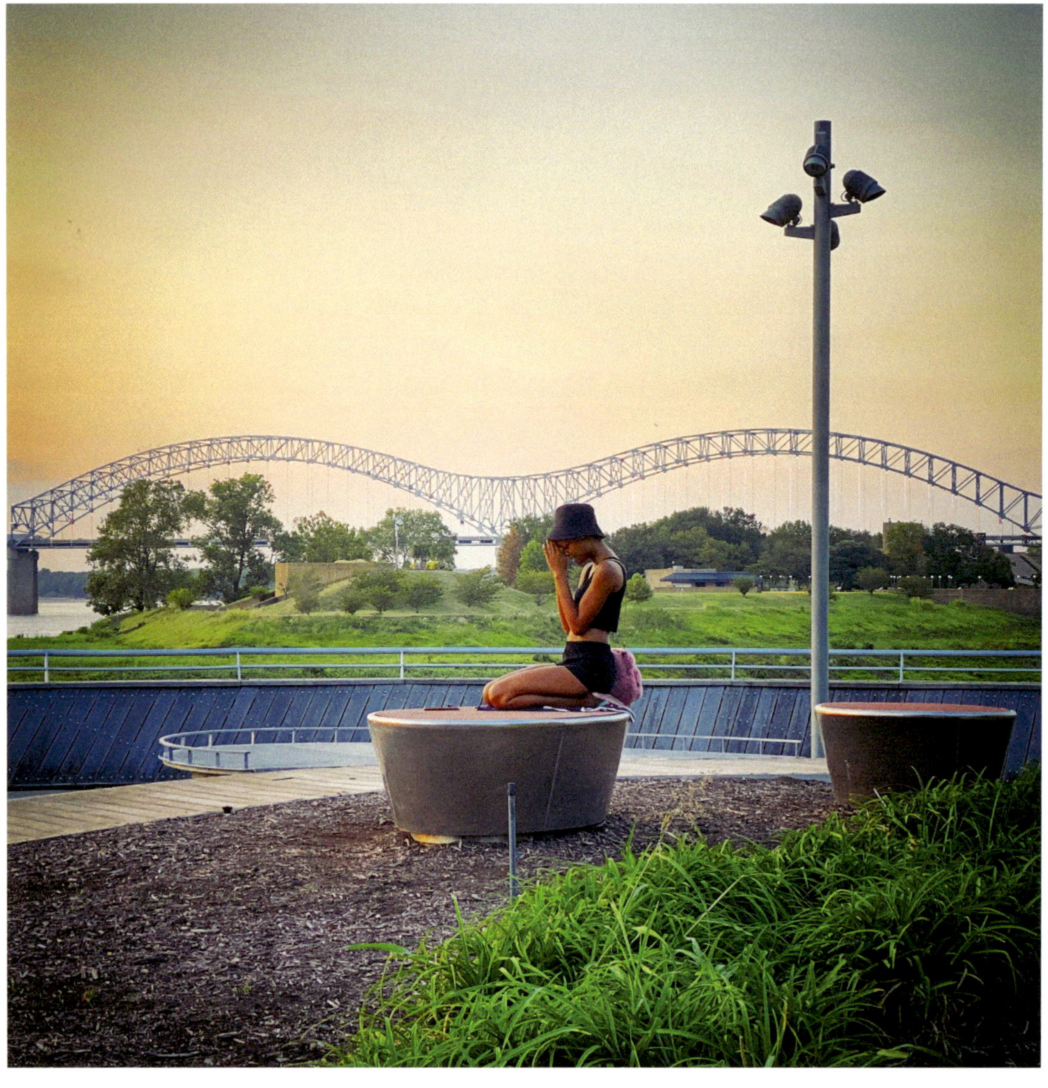

And nothing is left to be said or done but offer gratitude and thank you for taking this journey with me.

From Memphis with love,
Adam

Epilogue

I am indebted to many people for making this book happen. First and foremost, Jay Slater of Fonthill Media, for contacting me and offering to publish this edition of *Photographer's America*. Kena Smith, Fonthill Media's editor, suffered through more questions than anybody should. Hopefully, your next project is with someone who isn't such a Luddite and technophobe.

Three people gave direct assistance, and the world is a better place for them being in it. Kelly Haydon, Mike Kerr, and McKenzie Lyman gave me encouragement, time, and insights on how to make this far better than it would have been without their input. Oh, who am I kidding? I never would have crossed the finish line without their help. I hope they realize how appreciative I am for their support.

Early in the book, I mentioned that Memphis has an incredible community of photographers. I debated naming (Instagram) names here because I will inevitably omit and forget people. But one of the biggest reasons Memphis is my home is the incredible community of photographers in the town. I've lived in many places, but I've never seen—or been part of—a photography community like Memphis'.

It's no coincidence I asked Mike Kerr for help with this book's text. Not only is his Instagram page, @mikekerrmemphisphoto, filled wall-to-wall with incredible photography, but his captions are an encyclopedia of Memphis history. He is a constant source of inspiration and knowledge. Long may he run.

Memphis has incredible heritage and an abundance of abandoned homes and buildings (known as "bandos") to explore. @memphis_heritage and @rayofdecay explore each genre and (coincidentally) are both run by the same individual.

For exploring nature in Memphis and the surrounding areas, @aintitquaint can't be beaten.

For their ability to capture the 901, give the following a follow:

@deepcityvisuals
@reg2chill
@krystleplace
@hellcathaley
@ruderformssurvive
@sundayinmemphis
@_willpittman_
@amuricaphoto
@abstrac54321
@joeltrose

Every Memorial Day weekend, Memphis hosts Grind City Meet. It's a chance for photographers to get together and shoot around the town. I quickly became friends with people whose work on Instagram I had been admiring and envying. Whether you're a professional or amateur photographer, it's well worth your while to visit and take part. The event is run by @allyperkins and others and is now and forever dedicated to the memory of @webraw.